First World War
and Army of Occupation
War Diary
France, Belgium and Germany

58 DIVISION
Divisional Troops
Royal Army Medical Corps
2/3 Home Counties Field Ambulance
1 February 1917 - 29 May 1919

WO95/2997/6

The Naval & Military Press Ltd
www.nmarchive.com
Published in association with The National Archives

Published by

The Naval & Military Press Ltd

Unit 10 Ridgewood Industrial Park,
Uckfield, East Sussex,
TN22 5QE England
Tel: +44 (0) 1825 749494

www.naval-military-press.com
www.nmarchive.com

Contents

Document type	Place/Title	Date From	Date To
Heading	WO95/2997-6		
Heading	2-3rd (H.C) Field Ambnce 1915 Sep-1916 Feb And 1917 Feb-1919 Mar		
War Diary	War Diary By Lt Col J Barkley O.C. 2/3rd H. C Field Ambce		
War Diary	Remaisnil	01/02/1917	06/02/1917
War Diary	Le Souich	07/02/1917	07/02/1917
War Diary	Brevillers	07/02/1917	07/02/1917
War Diary	Le Souich	11/02/1917	11/02/1917
War Diary	Brevillers	11/02/1917	11/02/1917
War Diary	Le Souich	11/02/1917	11/02/1917
War Diary	Brevillers	12/02/1917	13/02/1917
War Diary	Le Souich	16/02/1917	16/02/1917
War Diary	Brevillers	17/02/1917	20/02/1917
War Diary	Humber Camp	21/02/1917	25/02/1917
Heading	War Diary Of Lt Col J Borkley Comdg 2/3rd Home Counties Field Ambulance From 1.3.17 To 25.3.17		
War Diary	Humbercamp	01/03/1917	25/03/1917
Heading	58th Divn. 2/3rd Home Counties F.A.		
War Diary	Grenas	31/03/1917	31/03/1917
War Diary	Ransart	01/04/1917	01/04/1917
War Diary	Bachimont	02/04/1917	05/04/1917
War Diary	Bus Les Artois	06/04/1917	09/04/1917
War Diary	Acheux	11/04/1917	24/04/1917
Heading	War Diary Of 2/3rd H C Fld Amb From 1/5/17 To 26/5/17		
War Diary	Acheux	01/05/1917	12/05/1917
War Diary	Achiet-Le-Grand	13/05/1917	15/05/1917
War Diary	Behagnies	15/05/1917	15/05/1917
War Diary	Behagnies	17/05/1917	26/05/1917
Heading	2/3rd Home Counties F. A. June 1917		
War Diary	Ervillers	01/06/1917	23/06/1917
War Diary	Bucquoy	24/06/1917	30/06/1917
Heading	War Diary 2/3rd H. C. Field Ambulance July 1917 Vol 6		
War Diary	Bucquoy	01/07/1917	07/07/1917
War Diary	Bus	07/07/1917	29/07/1917
War Diary	Wanquentin	30/07/1917	31/07/1917
Heading	War Diary Of 2/3rd H. C. Field Ambulance For The Month Of August 1917		
Miscellaneous	B.E.F. Summary Of Medical War Diaries Of 2/3rd H. C. F. A. 58th Div.		
War Diary	Wanquetin	04/08/1917	23/08/1917
War Diary	Lebbe Farm Poperinghe	25/08/1917	25/08/1917
War Diary	Lebbe Farm	26/08/1917	28/08/1917
War Diary	Duhallow Ads In The Line	29/08/1917	29/08/1917
War Diary	In The Line	30/08/1917	31/08/1917
War Diary	Moves And Transfer	25/08/1917	25/08/1917
War Diary	Moves	29/08/1917	29/08/1917
War Diary	Medical Arrangements	29/08/1917	29/08/1917

War Diary	Casualties R.A.M.C.	29/08/1917	29/08/1917
War Diary	Casualties R.A.M.C.	02/09/1917	02/09/1917
War Diary	Medical Arrangements	02/09/1917	02/09/1917
War Diary	Medical Arrangements	04/09/1917	04/09/1917
War Diary	Casualties R.A.M.C.	06/09/1917	06/09/1917
War Diary	Casualties R.A.M.C. Gas	07/09/1917	07/09/1917
War Diary	Casualties R.A.M.C.	08/09/1917	11/09/1917
War Diary	Medical Arrangements	15/09/1917	15/09/1917
War Diary	Casualties R.A.M.C.	15/09/1917	15/09/1917
Heading	War Diary Medical For Month Of September 2/3rd Home Counties Field Ambulance R.A.M.C. Vol 8		
War Diary	Sheet 28 C.25.a.3.0	01/09/1917	08/09/1917
War Diary	Sheet 28 C.25.d.3.0	09/09/1917	28/09/1917
War Diary	Gwent Farm Sheet 28 A.28.a.5.5	28/09/1917	30/09/1917
Miscellaneous	Summary Of Medical War Diaries Of 2/3rd H.C.F.A. 58th Div. 18th Corps. 5th Army		
War Diary	Moves And Transfer	25/08/1917	25/08/1917
War Diary	Moves	29/08/1917	29/08/1917
War Diary	Medical Arrangements	29/08/1917	29/08/1917
War Diary	Casualties R.A.M.C.	29/08/1917	29/08/1917
War Diary	Casualties R.A.M.C.	02/09/1917	02/09/1917
War Diary	Medical Arrangements	02/09/1917	02/09/1917
War Diary	Medical Arrangements	04/09/1917	04/09/1917
War Diary	Casualties R.A.M.C.	06/09/1917	06/09/1917
War Diary	Casualties R.A.M.C. Gas.	07/09/1917	07/09/1917
War Diary	Casualties R.A.M.C.	08/09/1917	11/09/1917
War Diary	Medical Arrangements	15/09/1917	15/09/1917
War Diary	Casualties R.A.M.C.	15/09/1917	15/09/1917
War Diary	Casualties R.A.M.C.	16/09/1917	16/09/1917
War Diary	Medical Arrangements Assistance	19/09/1917	19/09/1917
War Diary	Operations R.A.M.C.	20/09/1917	20/09/1917
War Diary	Medical Arrangements	20/09/1917	20/09/1917
War Diary	Medical Arrangements	22/09/1917	22/09/1917
War Diary	Operations Enemy	24/09/1917	24/09/1917
War Diary	Casualties R.A.M.C.	24/09/1917	24/09/1917
War Diary	Casualties A.S.C.	24/09/1917	24/09/1917
War Diary	Moves Detachment	24/09/1917	24/09/1917
War Diary	Medical Arrangements	25/09/1917	25/09/1917
War Diary	Operations Enemy	25/09/1917	25/09/1917
War Diary	Casualties R.A.M.C.	25/09/1917	25/09/1917
War Diary	Casualties A.S.C. Attached.	25/09/1917	25/09/1917
War Diary	Medical Arrangements	26/09/1917	26/09/1917
War Diary	Casualties R.A.M.C.	26/09/1917	26/09/1917
War Diary	Medical Arrangements	27/09/1917	27/09/1917
War Diary	Casualties	27/09/1917	27/09/1917
War Diary	Medical Arrangements	28/09/1917	28/09/1917
War Diary	Moves	28/09/1917	28/09/1917
War Diary	Casualties R.A.M.C.	16/09/1917	16/09/1917
War Diary	Medical Arrangements Assistance	19/09/1917	19/09/1917
War Diary	Operations R.A.M.C.	20/09/1917	20/09/1917
War Diary	Medical Arrangements	20/09/1917	20/09/1917
War Diary	Medical Arrangements	22/09/1917	22/09/1917
War Diary	Operations Enemy	24/09/1917	24/09/1917
War Diary	Casualties R.A.M.C.	24/09/1917	24/09/1917
War Diary	Casualties A.S.C Attached	24/09/1917	24/09/1917
War Diary	Moves Detachment	24/09/1917	24/09/1917

War Diary	Medical Arrangements	25/09/1917	25/09/1917
War Diary	Operations Enemy	25/09/1917	25/09/1917
War Diary	Casualties R.A.M.C.	25/09/1917	25/09/1917
War Diary	Casualties A.S.C Attached	25/09/1917	25/09/1917
War Diary	Medical Arrangements	26/09/1917	26/09/1917
War Diary	Casualties R.A.M.C.	26/09/1917	26/09/1917
War Diary	Medical Arrangements	27/09/1917	27/09/1917
War Diary	Casualties	27/09/1917	27/09/1917
War Diary	Medical Arrangements	28/09/1917	28/09/1917
War Diary	Moves	28/09/1917	28/09/1917
Heading	2/3rd Home Counties F. A. Oct 1917		
Heading	War Diary-Medical Of 2/3 Home Counties Field Ambulance R.A.M.C. T.F. October 1917		
War Diary	Gwent Farm Sheet 28 A 28.a.5.5	01/10/1917	01/10/1917
War Diary	Blanc Pignon Hazebrouck 5a 2 B. O.4	01/10/1917	21/10/1917
War Diary	Road Camp Sheet 27. L.1.a	22/10/1917	23/10/1917
War Diary	Gwent Farm Sheet 28 A 28a 5.5	24/10/1917	24/10/1917
War Diary	Sheet 28 C 19 C.3.0 Essex Farm	25/10/1917	27/10/1917
War Diary	Essex Farm Sheet 28 C.19.c 3.0	27/10/1917	31/10/1917
Heading	2/3rd Home Counties F.A Nov. 1917		
Heading	War Diary Of From November 1st 1917 To November 30th 1917 Vol 10		
War Diary	Sheet 28 C.19.c.3.0 Essex Farm	01/11/1917	14/11/1917
War Diary	Sheet 28 A.28.a.5.5	14/11/1917	14/11/1917
War Diary	Sheet 27 F.1.3.3.2 Porter Camp	14/11/1917	27/11/1917
War Diary	Lart Hazebrouck 5a 4.a 6.3	28/11/1917	30/11/1917
War Diary	Affringues Hazebrouck 5a 4.b.1.4.	30/11/1917	30/11/1917
Heading	2/3rd Home Counties F. A. Dec 1917		
War Diary	Hazebrouck 5a 4.B.1.4 Affringues	01/12/1917	06/12/1917
War Diary	Gwent Farm Sheet 28 A.28.a.5.5	06/12/1917	08/12/1917
War Diary	Essex Farm Sheet 28 C 19 C 3.0	08/12/1917	11/12/1917
War Diary	Gwent Farm Sheet G 28a 5.5	11/12/1917	11/12/1917
War Diary	Canada Farm Sheet 28.a.18.a 27	12/12/1917	31/12/1917
Heading	War Diary Of 2/3rd Home Counties Field Ambulance R.A.M.C. T. From January 1st 1918 To January 31st 1918		
War Diary	58 DRS Canada Fa Sheet A 18a 27	01/01/1918	07/01/1918
War Diary	58 DRS Sheet 27 C.10.c.1.9	08/01/1918	19/01/1918
War Diary	Central Camp	20/01/1918	20/01/1918
War Diary	Villers Brettoneux Sheet 62a 0.2 B0.7	21/01/1918	31/01/1918
Heading	War Diary Of 2/3rd Home Counties Field Ambulance R.A.M.C. T.F. From February 1st 1918 To February 28th 1918		
War Diary	Sheet 62d O.2.b.0.7	01/02/1918	06/02/1918
War Diary	Sheet 66e S.19.b.52 Villequier Aumont	06/02/1918	20/02/1918
War Diary	Marest Dampcourt Sht 66c L.7.b.3.0	27/02/1918	28/02/1918
Heading	War Diary Of 2/3rd Home Counties Field Ambulance R.A.M.C. T. From 1st March 1918 To 31st March 1918		
War Diary	Marest Dampcourt Sht 70e L.7.b.3.0	01/03/1918	20/03/1918
War Diary	Chauny	21/03/1918	21/03/1918
War Diary	Villequier Aumont Sht 66c. S.19.c.5.2	21/03/1918	22/03/1918
War Diary	Marest Sht 70e L.1.c.6.2	23/03/1918	24/03/1918
War Diary	Varennes	24/03/1918	25/03/1918
War Diary	Nampcel	26/03/1918	27/03/1918
War Diary	Hautebraye	28/03/1918	31/03/1918

Heading	War Diary Of 2/3rd Home Counties Field Ambulance R.A.M.C. T. From April 1st 1918 To April 30th 1918		
War Diary	Hautebraye	01/04/1918	05/04/1918
War Diary	43 Rue Porte Parts Amiens	06/04/1918	28/04/1918
War Diary	Crouy	28/04/1918	29/04/1918
War Diary	Buigny L'abbe	29/04/1918	30/04/1918
Heading	War Diary Of 2/3rd Home Counties Field Ambulance R.A.M.C. T. From May 1st 1918 To May 31st 1918 Vol 16		
War Diary	Buigny L'abbe	02/05/1918	06/05/1918
War Diary	St Gratien Sht 628 B.26.B.6.9	06/05/1918	16/05/1918
War Diary	Vadencourt	16/05/1918	31/05/1918
Heading	War Diary Of 2/3rd Home Counties Field Ambulance R.A.M.C. T. From June 1st 1918 To June 30th 1918 Vol 17		
War Diary	Vadencourt	01/06/1918	01/06/1918
War Diary	St Gratien Wood Sht 62d B.26.b.6.9	02/06/1918	11/06/1918
War Diary	St Pierre a Gouy	11/06/1918	17/06/1918
War Diary	Sht 62d B.26.b	17/06/1918	18/06/1918
War Diary	Sht 62d. D.13.d.8.2	18/06/1918	20/06/1918
War Diary	Sht 62d B.26.b	20/06/1918	30/06/1918
Heading	War Diary Of 2/3rd Home Counties Field Ambulance R.A.M.C. T. From 1st July 1918 To 31st July 1918 Vol 18		
War Diary	Sht 62d B.26. B.6.9	01/07/1918	01/07/1918
War Diary	Sht 62d C.20.b.4.2 Franvillers Wood	01/07/1918	31/07/1918
Heading	War Diary Of 2/3rd Home Counties Field Ambulance R.A.M.C. T. From August 1st 1918 To August 31st 1918		
War Diary	Round Wood Sht 62d C.20.b.4.2	01/08/1918	03/08/1918
War Diary	Vignacourt	03/08/1918	06/08/1918
War Diary	St Gratien Wood Sht 62d. B.20.b	15/08/1918	23/08/1918
War Diary	Sheet 62d St. Gratien Wood B 20.b.	24/08/1918	24/08/1918
War Diary	I.30.a.6.6	25/08/1918	25/08/1918
War Diary	J. 24.b.	25/08/1918	30/08/1918
War Diary	L.10.a	30/08/1918	30/08/1918
War Diary	Sht 62d. L.10.a	30/08/1918	31/08/1918
War Diary	Sht 62c. A.21.b.	31/08/1918	31/08/1918
Heading	War Diary Of 2/3rd Home Counties Field Ambulance R.A.M.C. T. From Sept 1st To Sept 30th 1918		
War Diary	Sht 62c. A.21.b Maricourt	01/09/1918	06/09/1918
War Diary	Sht 62c. C.20.a.9.1	07/09/1918	07/09/1918
War Diary	D.15.c.0.5	07/09/1918	08/09/1918
War Diary	E.14.a.8.8	08/09/1918	11/09/1918
War Diary	Sheet 62c. E.14.a.8.8	12/09/1918	24/09/1918
War Diary	S.28.d.6.4 Sht 578	24/09/1918	26/09/1918
War Diary	Villers Au Bois	27/09/1918	30/09/1918
Heading	War Diary Of 2/3rd Home Counties Field Ambulance R.A.M.C. T. From 1st October To 31st October 1918		
War Diary	Sht 44 B. Q. 34.a.2.5	01/10/1918	13/10/1918
War Diary	Sht 44 B R. 8. Cent	13/10/1918	19/10/1918
War Diary	Sht 44a. O 21.a Cent	20/10/1918	20/10/1918
War Diary	Sht 44a P 6.a.9.3	21/10/1918	21/10/1918
War Diary	Sht 44a L21.a.7.0	22/10/1918	31/10/1918
Heading	War Diary Of 2/3rd Home Counties Field Ambulance R.A.M.C. T. From Nov. 1st To Nov 30th 1918		

War Diary	Bersee	01/11/1918	07/11/1918
War Diary	Aix	07/11/1918	10/11/1918
War Diary	Rumegies	10/11/1918	11/11/1918
War Diary	Peruwelz	11/11/1918	30/11/1918
Heading	War Diary Of 2/3rd Home Counties Field Ambulance R.A.M.C. T.F. From December 1st 1918 To December 31st 1918 Vol 23		
War Diary	Peruwelz	07/12/1918	29/12/1918
Heading	War Diary Of 2/3rd Home Counties Field Ambulance R.A.M.C. T. From January 1st 1919 To January 31st 1919 Vol 24		
War Diary	Peruwelz	12/01/1919	24/01/1919
Heading	War Diary Of 2/3rd Home Counties Field Ambulance R.A.M.C. February 1st To February 28th 1919		
War Diary	Peruwelz	03/02/1919	28/02/1919
Heading	War Diary 2/3rd Home Counties Field Ambulance March 1919 Vol 26		
War Diary	Peruwelz	02/03/1919	04/03/1919
War Diary	Chapelle A Wattines	04/03/1919	30/03/1919
Heading	War Diary 2/3rd Home Counties Field Ambulance April 1919 Vol 27		
War Diary	Chapelle-A-Wattines	16/04/1919	30/04/1919
Heading	War Diary 2/3 Home Counties Field Ambulance May 1919 Vol 28		
War Diary	Chapelle-A-Wattines	02/05/1919	29/05/1919
Miscellaneous	2/3rd. Home Counties Field Ambulance RAMC, T.		

58TH DIVISION

2-3RD (H.C) FIELD AMBNCE

~~FEB 1917 DEC 1918~~

1915 SEP — 1916 FEB
and
1917 FEB — 1919 MAR

58

58th Div

1+d/99+

Vol 1

WAR DIARY

BY

LT COL. J. Barkley, O.C., 2/3rd H C Field Ambce

26 - 2 - 1917

Army Form C. 2118.

Instructions regarding War Diaries and Intelligence Summaries are contained in F. S. Regs., Part II. and the Staff Manual respectively. Title Pages will be prepared in manuscript.

WAR DIARY
or
INTELLIGENCE SUMMARY
(Erase heading not required.)

Place	Date	Hour	Summary of Events and Information	Remarks and references to Appendices
REMAISNIL	1/2/17	10 hrs	3718 L Cpl WOODARD. E. sent to C.C.S. DOULLENS suffering from a fractured right arm. Instructions received from 58th D.H.Q. that the sick of the 2/1st, 2/2nd, 2/3rd Bns LONDON REGTS and 293rd F.A. Brigade are to be evacuated by this unit to the C.C.S. DOULLENS.	
"		19 hrs	Notification received from A.D.M.S. 58th Div. that seven Motor Ambulances and two motor cycles with drivers were due to leave ABBEVILLE at 15 hrs, en route for destination here.	
"	2/2/17	9.45 hrs	Pair of horses in B. Section G.S. Wagon took fright at a thrashing machine and bolted. The wagon is damaged and unable to be worked.	
"	3/2/17	11 hrs	Two Officers (CAPT CUMMINGS and CAPT DAVIES) and thirty other ranks left by motor lorry to the C.O. 1/1st NORTH MIDLAND FIELD AMBULANCE stationed at D 20 CENTRAL. Routine Orders 58th (LONDON) Div. dated Feb. 3. 1917. No 105 SICK EVACUATION "The 2/3 H.C. FIELD AMBULANCE will collect from R.E, A.S.C. and Divisional H.Q. Troops and also the 293rd Brigade R.F.A.	
"	4/2/17	14 hrs	Seven motor ambulances arrived, consisting of 5 Siddley Deasy + 2 Ford cars and one Douglas motor cycle. They were accompanied by 12 N.C.O.s and men. Order from A.D.M.S. 58th Div. "Please instruct CAPT. W.W MAXWELL of your unit to report to the office of the D.D.M.S. 18th CORPS on Feb. 8th 1917 for the purpose of carrying out the duties of M.O. i/c troops at CORPS H.Q. for a period of 30 days. CAPT MAXWELL will be shown as still in the strength of your UNIT on the weekly nominal role of officers submitted to D.G.M.S. G.H.Q 2nd Echelon. 3rd Army as D.D.M.S. 18th Corps.	
"	5/2/17	10.30	Court of inquiry held on damaged G.S. Wagon. find no blame attached to driver.	

Instructions regarding War Diaries and Intelligence Summaries are contained in F. S. Regs., Part II. and the Staff Manual respectively. Title Pages will be prepared in manuscript.

WAR DIARY
or
INTELLIGENCE SUMMARY
(Erase heading not required.)

Army Form C. 2118.

Place	Date	Hour	Summary of Events and Information	Remarks and references to Appendices
REMAISNIL	6/7/17	10 hrs	The Field Ambulance left REMAISNIL and marched via DOULLENS and LUCHEUX to LE SOUICH	
LE SOUICH		16.30 hrs	Arrived at LE SOUICH. CAPT. W.W. MAXWELL left to join CORPS H.Q. to-day.	
LE SOUICH	7/7/17	15 hrs	'A' and 'B' Sections and Field Ambulance H.Q. left LE SOUICH for BREVILLERS.	
		10 hrs	'C' Section took over the Hospital at LE SOUICH. CAPT MATTHEWS & CAPT MALKIN with tent sub-divisions and some bearers as general duty men of 'C' Section remained at the hospital at LE SOUICH as the Staff.	
BREVILLERS	7/7/17	15.30 hrs	Field Amb. H.Q. & 'A' & 'B' Sections arrived at BREVILLERS and took over the chateau there.	
LE SOUICH	11/7/17	16 hrs	Visit by D.D.M.S. XVIII Corps to HOSPITAL at LE SOUICH	
BREVILLERS	11/7/17		Two Officers (MAJOR FULTON & CAPT MALKIN) and thirty other ranks sent for duty with 46th Div. Two Officers (CAPT. CUMMINGS & CAPT DAVIES) and thirty other ranks returned from duty with 46th Div.	
LE SOUICH	11/7/17	18 hrs	CAPT. DAVIES replaced CAPT MALKIN for duty at the hospital LE SOUICH.	
BREVILLERS	12/7/17	22 hrs	Six men rejoined Unit from England.	
	13/7/17		One man sent for duty with D.D.M.S. XVIII Corps.	
LE SOUICH	16/7/17	17 hrs	'B' Section took over the hospital at LE SOUICH from 'C' Section. Thaw set in.	
BREVILLERS	17/7/17		Two Officers (Capt. MATTHEWS & LIEUT. MAILE) and thirty other ranks left for duty with the 46th Division.	

Instructions regarding War Diaries and Intelligence Summaries are contained in F. S. Regs., Part II. and the Staff Manual respectively. Title Pages will be prepared in manuscript.

WAR DIARY
or
INTELLIGENCE SUMMARY

(Erase heading not required.)

Army Form C. 2118.

Place	Date	Hour	Summary of Events and Information	Remarks and references to Appendices
BREVILLERS	18/2/17	9pm	Received order from ADMS 58th Divn to hand over Hospital at Le Souich and billets at BREVILLERS to O/C 1/1 W. RIDING F AMB. and to take over hospital as MDS at HUMBERCAMP and ADS at BAILLEULVAL. Advance party proceeded to HUMBERCAMP + BAILLEULVAL	[illegible]
"	19/2/17	9am	A Sec Horse Ambulance wagon injured on frozen road between BREVILLERS + LE SOUICH. [illegible] destroyed, stanchion broken, rim of wheel broken. This was due to [illegible] slip into gully when passing another ambulance on frozen road, the four horses dragged the wagon against an overhanging [illegible].	[illegible]
"	20/2	8am	Detached party	
"	20/2	8am	Main body of unit moved to HUMBERCAMP. Detached party commanded by Lieut MAILE joined at 10am at HUMBERCAMP. Took over hospital and advanced dressing station. [illegible] in Section C. Inspected advanced dressing station and found in clean and in fair condition. Capt MATTHEWS evacuated to ST POL DIPHTHERIA	[illegible]
HUMBERCAMP	21/2		Inspected three Bearer posts or collecting posts. [illegible] wheeled stretcher being [illegible] by a very long carry, advised removal by road through [BERLES?] [illegible] the ploughed land, advised removal [illegible] be removed to (Cuppa Tunnel) [illegible]. R31C19 might with advantage also be closed as [illegible]. R26 85 might with advantage [illegible] there is no work done there as it is in advance of the RAP R25 [illegible]. Forty one patients were transferred to MDS at HUMBERCAMP [illegible] from LESOUICH. Eight fresh cases admitted 1 transferred to CCS [illegible]. Gas alarm 8pm	[illegible]
	22/2		Eleven cases admitted. 2 to CCS transfer and seven discharged to duty. [illegible]	
	23/2		Nineteen cases admitted two transferred wounded to CCS. [illegible]	
	22/2		DMS, DDMS XVIII Corps, ADMS + DADMS 58th DIVN visited HUMBERCAMP	
	23/2		Operation order No 3 ~~[illegible]~~ by ADMS 58 Divn received. Capt [illegible] [illegible] to ST POL (German measles)	[illegible]

3349 Wt. W14957/M90 750,000 11/16 J.B.C. & A. Forms/C.2118/12.

Instructions regarding War Diaries and Intelligence Summaries are contained in F. S. Regs., Part II. and the Staff Manual respectively. Title Pages will be prepared in manuscript.

WAR DIARY
or
INTELLIGENCE SUMMARY
(Erase heading not required.)

Army Form C. 2118.

Place	Date	Hour	Summary of Events and Information	Remarks and references to Appendices
HUMBER CAMP	25/2	3.15 am	Signal M60 d/25 received	
		4 am	Notified Major FULTON O/C Section B at advanced dressing station to hold himself in readiness to move. At main dressing station kept A Section in reserve and packed & parked B Sec wagons, animals ordered to move at 5 am	
		10 am	Signal to A.D.M.S. 58th Div whether we should evacuate patients or not	
		12.45 pm	Order received cancelling M60 d/25. Withdrew horses & limbered wagons from advanced dressing station	
		3 pm	A.D.M.S. 58th Div inspected advanced dressing station W4 a.3.7 and R 35 a 4.7. The latter was taken over by 2/2 Home Counties Field Ambulance. The weather has been dull ever since 17th Feby so ~~that~~ that no aeroplanes were visible until this afternoon.	

James Barkley
LIEUT. COL.
O.C. 2nd/3rd HOME COUNTIES
FIELD AMBULANCE R.A.M.C.

2449 Wt. W14957/M90 750,000 1/16 J.B.C. & A. Forms/C.2118/12.

Medical.

140/2042

Mar. 1917

Vol II

Confidential

War Diary

of

Lt Col J. Barkley

Cmdg 2/3rd HOME COUNTIES FIELD AMBULANCE

from 1-3-17 to 25.3.17.

Instructions regarding War Diaries and Intelligence Summaries are contained in F. S. Regs., Part II. and the Staff Manual respectively. Title Pages will be prepared in manuscript.

WAR DIARY
or
INTELLIGENCE SUMMARY

(Erase heading not required.)

Army Form C. 2118.

Place	Date	Hour	Summary of Events and Information	Remarks and references to Appendices
HUMBERCAMP	1-3-17		GAS ALERT - on -	
			DAILY STATE Patients admitted 11 - transferred 4 - discharged 11 Remaining 78	
			4 men reinforcements arrived from BASE. LtCDM	
"	2-3-17		GAS ALERT - on	
			DAILY STATE Patients admitted 17 - transferred 7 - discharged 9 Remaining 79. LtCDM	
"	3-3-17		GAS ALERT on	
			DAILY STATE Patients admitted 13 - transferred 3 - discharged 12 - Remaining 77.	
			LIEUT MAILE returned to Headquarters from BAILLEUVAL. - CAPT. DAVIES proceeded to BAILLEUVAL for duty - LtCDM	
"	4-3-17		GAS ALERT on	
			DAILY STATE Patients admitted 14 - transferred 10 - discharged 14 - Remaining 67. LtCDM	
"	5-3-17		GAS ALERT on	
			DAILY STATE Patients admitted 26 - transferred 13 - discharged 18 - Remaining 62	
		9 AM	Operation order No 6 received from ADMS re evacuating A.D.S. BAILLEUVAL & taking over A.D.S. BERLES from 46th DIVISION. 1 officer & other ranks + 1 Motor ambulance to remain at BAILLEUVAL to form a Collecting post.	
		5 PM	Signal from ADMS received - "movements of units cancelled pending further instructions" LtCDM	
"	6-3-17		GAS ALERT on	
			DAILY STATE Patients admitted 20 - transferred 5 - discharged 8 - Remaining 69	
		9 AM.	Signal from ADMS - "operation order No 6 to be completed by 12 noon to-day".	
		4.10 PM	Signal from O.C 'B' Section stating move completed	
			BERLES shelled with GAS SHELLS - 2 men admitted to Hospital suffering from GAS POISONING. LtCDM	
"	7-3-17.		GAS ALERT on	
			DAILY STATE Patients admitted 21 - transferred 13 - discharged 3 - Remaining 74 -	
		9.30 AM	3 ENEMY SHELLS fell near the Hospital (HUMBERCAMP) - 2 failed to explode - no damage done to Hospital	
			CAPT. MALKIN rejoined unit having been discharged from hospital ST. POL LtCDM	
"	8-3-17		GAS ALERT - on	
			DAILY STATE - Patients admitted 14 - transferred 6 - discharged 6 - Remaining 76	

2449 Wt. W14957/M90 750,000 1/16 J.B.C. & A. Forms/C.2118/12.

Army Form C. 2118.

Instructions regarding War Diaries and Intelligence Summaries are contained in F. S. Regs., Part II. and the Staff Manual respectively. Title Pages will be prepared in manuscript.

WAR DIARY
or
INTELLIGENCE SUMMARY

(Erase heading not required.)

Place	Date	Hour	Summary of Events and Information	Remarks and references to Appendices
HUMBERCAMP	8 3 17 (contd)	9 30 AM	C.O proceeded to BERLES & met D.A.D.M.S	
		3.35 PM	ADMS visited Hospital (HUMBERCAMP)	
			1 man transferred to HAVRE as under age for service overseas. Lt CDM	
"	9 3 17		GAS ALERT on	
			DAILY STATE - Patients admitted 13 - transferred 6 - discharged 7 - Remaining 76 Lt CDM	
"	10 3 17		GAS ALERT on	
			DAILY STATE - Patients admitted 20 - transferred 10 - discharged 10 - Remaining 76	
		3 PM	DDMS XVIII CORPS visited hospital. Lt CDM	
"	11 3 17		GAS ALERT on	
			DAILY STATE Patients admitted 17 - transferred 5 - discharged 9 - Remaining 79	
			ADMS admitted to Hospital. C.O. took over duties of ADMS temporarily	
			Operation order No 8 received from ADMS re taking over Bearer posts on MONCHY - HANNESCAMPS - Rd Lt CDM	
"	12 3 17		GAS ALERT on	
			DAILY STATE - Patients admitted 20 - transferred 2 - discharged 9 - Remaining 90.	
			C.O visited ADMS' office at BAVINCOURT Lt CDM	
"	13 3 17		GAS ALERT on	
			DAILY STATE - Patients admitted 25 - transferred 5 - discharged 9 - Remaining 101.	
		6.45 AM	Operation order No 9 received from ADMS re taking over an A.D.S at BIENVILLERS.	
		2 PM	1 officer (CAPT. MALKIN) & 30 other ranks proceeded to BIENVILLERS.	
		4 PM	ADS BIENVILLERS taken over.	
		5 PM	Secret communication from ADMS re an attack by our troops which was to take place at 5 AM on 14-3-17- Lt CDM	
"	14 3 17		GAS ALERT on	
			DAILY STATE - Patients admitted 24 - transferred 6 - discharged 14 - Remaining 106.	
		10 AM	C.O. visited ADMS' office.	
		4 PM	Secret order received - re - S.O.S. signal of the 3rd ARMY	
			1 officer (CAPT. HARDWICK) & 16 other ranks of the 2/1st HOME COUNTIES FIELD AMBULANCE reported for duty to O.C. ADS. BERLES. This party proceeded to BAILLEUVAL & took over Collecting post there from CAPT. DAVIES who proceeded to BIENVILLERS ADS for duty Lt CDM	

2449 Wt. W14957/M90 750,000 1/16 J.B.C. & A. Forms/C.2118/12.

Army Form C. 2118.

WAR DIARY
or
~~INTELLIGENCE SUMMARY~~
(Erase heading not required.)

Instructions regarding War Diaries and Intelligence Summaries are contained in F. S. Regs., Part II. and the Staff Manual respectively. Title Pages will be prepared in manuscript.

Place	Date	Hour	Summary of Events and Information	Remarks and references to Appendices
HUMBERCAMP	15-3-17		GAS ALERT on DAILY STATE – Patients admitted 33 – transferred 12 – discharged 12 – Remaining 115. McCDM	
"	16 3 17		GAS ALERT on DAILY STATE – Patients admitted 16 – transferred 11 – discharged 15 – Remaining 102 – DDMS XVIII CORPS visited Hospital McCDM	
"	17 3 17		GAS ALERT on – Fine sunny day – Roads drying up fast. DAILY STATE – Patients admitted 27 – transferred 4 – discharged 19 – Remaining 111 Secret order from A.D.M.S — "one complete section shall remain packed & ready to move – remaining sections to carry on with their present duties until further orders". 2/3rd HOME COUNTIES FIELD AMBULANCE attached to 173rd BRIGADE –	
		2 PM.	C.O. visited the A.D.S BIENVILLERS – Inspected Bearer posts around HANNESCAMPS – Here news came through to the effect that MONCHY-AU-BOIS had been evacuated by the GERMANS & was occupied by our troops. A.D.S BERLES visited & then MONCHY – in order to see what arrangements could be made for the evacuation of sick & wounded from the new line – The road from BERLES to MONCHY was found impassible, & the village of MONCHY absolutely destroyed – only heaps of stones representing the sites of what were once houses — By the time MONCHY had been reached, darkness came on & so the C.O. decided to revisit the place as soon as it was daylight. McCDM	
"	18 3 17		GAS ALERT on – Fine sunny day – DAILY STATE – Patients admitted 15 – transferred 10 – discharged 11 – Remaining 98	
		9 AM	Letter from ADMS stating — Present situation — "58th Divisional line now extends from BOIRY BECQUERELLE to St LEGER MILL." C.O. visited RANSART – MONCHY district – explosion craters were ~~——~~ found at most cross roads especially near ADINFER & BOIRY St RECTRUDE – On MONCHY–RANSART road quantities of equipment were found strewn about as if the enemy had been caught unawares sometime. Wanton destruction was noticed everywhere – Houses destroyed – Fruit trees cut down etc. An enemy dug out fitted up for Medical purposes was found – It had accomodation for about 20 lying down cases – a quantity of dressings was found – also many packets of white powder for the prevention of cholera & a large quantity of Iodoform gauze & a few splints. This dug out was probably a R.A.P. BOIRY St RECTRUDE was found suitable for an A.D.S & the site decided on was the ~~——~~ SUGAR FACTORY. The 173rd BRIGADE was in touch with the enemy at St LEGER. McCDM	

2449 Wt. W14957/M90 750,000 1/16 J.B.C. & A. Forms/C.2118/12.

Army Form C. 2118.

Instructions regarding War Diaries and Intelligence Summaries are contained in F. S. Regs., Part II. and the Staff Manual respectively. Title Pages will be prepared in manuscript.

WAR DIARY
or
~~INTELLIGENCE SUMMARY~~
(Erase heading not required.)

Place	Date	Hour	Summary of Events and Information	Remarks and references to Appendices
HUMBERCAMP	19.3.17	6 AM	GAS ALERT off. – weather overcast – Several showers of rain during afternoon & evening.	
			DAILY STATE – Patients admitted – 30 – transferred 1 – discharged 42 – Remaining – 86.	
			ADS BIENVILLERS transferred to RANSART & thence later to SUGAR FACTORY – BOIRY ST. RECTRUDE	
		12 noon	ADS BERLES transferred to BAILLEUVAL & there to await further orders.	
			Method of evacuating sick & wounded from the line near BOYELLES as follows — From R.A.P.s by hand stretchers & wheeled stretchers to BOISLEUX-AU-MONT – thence by horse ambulance to A.D.S. BOIRY ST RECTRUDE. Thence by Motor ambulance to ADINFER – thence by wheeled stretcher to SHRAPNEL CORNER near BELLACOURT & from there by Motor ambulance to Field Ambulance at HUMBERCAMP. Field ambulance evacuates to Nos 20 & 43 C.C.S. WARLINCOURT.	
			New ADMS – Col. J W H HOUGHTON – A.M.S. lcOM	
"	20.3.17		GAS ALERT off	
			DAILY STATE – Patients admitted –	
			58th Division transferred from XVIII ~~Corps~~ CORPS to VII CORPS.	
			ADMS visited Field Ambulance.	
			C.O visited BOIRY ST RECTRUDE	
		5 PM	Orders received from ADMS – 'The section of Field Ambulance at BAILLEUVAL will proceed to SUGAR FACTORY – BOIRY ST RECTRUDE at daybreak & on arrival at this site will open a Second A.D.S. if occasion demands – lcOM	
"	21.3.17	6 AM	GAS ALERT on	
			DAILY STATE – Patients admitted 26 – transferred 6 – discharged 16 – Remaining ~~#~~ 101 –	
			ADS BAILLEUVAL transferred to BOIRY ST RECTRUDE – CAPT MAXWELL & 7 other ranks remained at BAILLEUVAL to form a collecting post.	
		10 PM.	Despatch from ADMS – Divisional boundary will now be as follows —— NORTHERN BOUNDARY – LABRET (inclusive) – BAILLEU ~~[illegible]~~ MONT (exclusive) RANSART (exclusive) HENDECOURT (inclusive) —— SOUTHERN BOUNDARY – HUMBERCAMP – BIENVILLERS – MONCHY – DOUCHY & AYETTE (all inclusive) MOYENVILLE (exclusive) — WESTERN BOUNDARY – SAULTY – GAUDIEMPRE (both exclusive)	
			DHQ remains at BAVINCOURT. – The party at present at BAILLEUVAL will be withdrawn & posted to ADS BERLES. lcOM	
	22/3/17		GAS ALERT on – weather very changeable – intervals of sunshine & then snow	
			DAILY STATE. Patients admitted 35 – transferred 13 – discharged 23 – Remaining 97	
			C.O visited BOIRY. Party at BAILLEUVAL transferred to ADS BERLES – lcOM	
	23/3/17		GAS ALERT on – weather fine but cold – Roads still very muddy.	
			DAILY STATE – Patients admitted 36 – transferred 9 – discharged 3 – Remaining 130 lcOM	

2449 Wt. W14957/M90 750,000 1/16 J.B.C. & A. Forms/C.2118/12.

Instructions regarding War Diaries and Intelligence Summaries are contained in F. S. Regs., Part II. and the Staff Manual respectively. Title Pages will be prepared in manuscript.

WAR DIARY
or
~~INTELLIGENCE SUMMARY~~
(Erase heading not required.)

Army Form C. 2118.

Place	Date	Hour	Summary of Events and Information	Remarks and references to Appendices
HUMBERCAMP	23/3/17 (Contd.)	4 PM.	ADMS visited hospital –	
			C.O. visited A.D.S. BOIRY McDM	
″	24/3/17		GAS ALERT on. Fine sunny day – cold wind – Frost last night – Roads drying up –	
			DAILY STATE – Patients admitted – 9 – transferred – 12 – discharged 24 – Remaining – 88	
			NOTES FOR WAR DIARY received from O/C ADS BOIRY	
			19th March 1917 – Reconnoitred sites for collecting posts in connection with ADS at BOIRY St RECTRUDE – very wet night – coming back road blocked all night by 'B' battery 291st BRIGRADE R.F.A. between RANSART & BELLACOURT.	
			20th March 1917 – 'C' Section under CAPT MAIKIN moved up from BIENVILLERS & opened ADS at SUGAR FACTORY on the outskirts of BOIRY St RECTRUDE – very wet day – all wells blown up & most cross roads	
			21st March 1917 'C' section settling in – Fine but snow during night of 20–21st – Got orders at midnight to move B Section up to BOIRY & moved accordingly in two detachments owing to shortage of horses via RANSART & ADINFER	
			22nd March 1917 – Improving camp – constructing latrines, cookhouses – washhouse & clearing out German dugouts –	
			23rd March 1917 – visited stretcher post at S11 a 1.0 & arranged new collecting post at S 29. a 9.1 with sheet 51B SW 3 Snow last night & sharp frost – Improving Camp	
			C.O visited ADS with ADMS	
		3 PM.	Operation order No 11 received re "174 Brigade relieving 173 Brigade in trenches commencing to-night" –	
		3.15 PM	Message from ADMS – "(British Armies in FRANCE will adopt Summer time at 11 PM on 24th instant" – at that moment clocks will be advanced one hour & 11 PM will become midnight" (wire repeated for information) McDM	
″	25/3/17		GAS ALERT on – weather – very fine sunny day – warm –	
			Daily State – Patients admitted – 39 transferred – 16 – discharged 24 Remaining – 92	
		3 PM.	'B' Section returned from BOIRY St RECTRUDE – 'A' Section replaced 'B' Section at A.D.S. BOIRY St RECTRUDE. McDM	

J Barkley
LIEUT. COL.
O.C. 2nd/3rd HOME COUNTIES
FIELD AMBULANCE R.A.M.C.

April 1917

S

58th Div.

140/2086.

2/3rd Home Counties F. A.

Instructions regarding War Diaries and Intelligence Summaries are contained in F. S. Regs., Part II. and the Staff Manual respectively. Title Pages will be prepared in manuscript.

WAR DIARY
or
INTELLIGENCE SUMMARY
(Erase heading not required.)

Army Form C. 2118.

2/3 HC Fd Amb
Vol 3

3rd HOME COUNTIES FIELD AMBULANCE R.A.M.C. No. — Date —

Place	Date	Hour	Summary of Events and Information	Remarks and references to Appendices
GRENAS	31.3.17		LIEUT MAILE with an advance party of 1 NCO & 9 men proceeded to RANSART to arrange billets with the equipment of one section — The horses returned to HUMBERCAMPS the same night. LCADMS	
RANSART	1.4.17		C.O proceeded to BACHIMONT to inspect accommodation & found the advance party of the 2/2 HOME COUNTIES FIELD AMBULANCE already in the place taking over the Hospital there — C.O then proceeded to ADMS office at FROHEN LE GRAND & was told that the 2/3rd HOME COUNTIES FIELD AMBULANCE was to take over at BACHIMONT the next day. The AMBULANCE arrived at RANSART. Very cold day — sleet & snow — CAPT MAXWELL with 10 other ranks proceeded to No 43 CCS for a course of instruction. LCGM	
BACHIMONT	2.4.17	9AM	LIEUT MAILE with 6 other ranks proceeded to BACHIMONT as an advance party & arrived at noon — The AMBULANCE arrived at 6PM & took over the CHATEAU as a hospital — Very cold day — Snow — Some equipment was left behind at RANSART — a rear party was left in charge of this. — CAPT MALLINSON detailed for duty at ~~[illegible]~~ BOUQUE MAISON ~~and~~ to report to Town Major. LCGM	
BACHIMONT	3.4.17		Spent getting Hospital into working order. Snowing — very cold day. LCGM	

2449 Wt. W14957/M90 750,000 1/16 J.B.C. & A. Forms/C.2118/12.

Army Form C. 2118.

WAR DIARY
or
~~INTELLIGENCE~~ SUMMARY
(Erase heading not required.)

Instructions regarding War Diaries and Intelligence Summaries are contained in F. S. Regs., Part II. and the Staff Manual respectively. Title Pages will be prepared in manuscript.

Place	Date	Hour	Summary of Events and Information	Remarks and references to Appendices
BACHIMONT	4.4.17		Operation order No 15A received from ADMS – "The O.C. 2/3rd HOME COUNTIES FIELD AMBULANCE will detail an advance party with medical equipment, to proceed by busses on the 5/4/17 with the 175 Brigade. The 2/3rd H C FIELD AMBULANCE (less advance party) will move in two marches to BUS LES ARTOIS on the 5/4/17 halting for the night at AUTHIEULE." LCOM	
BACHIMONT	5.4.17	9 AM	LIEUT MALE with 19 patients + an advance party of NCO's + men proceeded by Motor Bus to BUS. LES ARTOIS – + took over the Hospital from the rear party of the 21st FIELD AMBULANCE. LIEUT POOLE proceeded to AUTHIEULE with the Cooks Limber – to do the billeting there.	
		9.30 am	The AMBULANCE proceeded to AUTHIEULE + arrived there at 8 PM. CAPT MAXWELL rejoined unit. A rear party was left at BACHIMONT to clean up. CAPT. MALKIN rejoined unit. LCOM	
BUS LES ARTOIS	6.4.17		The AMBULANCE arrived here at 2 PM. The 2/2 H C. FIELD AMBULANCE also arrived + both AMBULANCES remained in the Hospital for the night. One of our horses (heavy draught) was shot on the road by the Vet. LCOM	
"	7.4.17		The 2/2 H.C. FIELD AMBULANCE left – for BERTRANCOURT. LCOM	
"	9.4.17		The AMBULANCE moved to ACHEUX + took over CORPS COLLECTING STATION with 132 patients from 2/3rd WEST RIDING FIELD AMBULANCE – CAPTS. MAXWELL + DAVIES + one tent subdivision proceeded to No. 4 C.C.S for a course of instruction – CAPT MALKIN detailed as M.O. to the 2/12 LONDON REGT. LCOM	
ACHEUX	11.4.17		LIEUT. MALE + 7 other ranks proceeded to point P. 17 a. + took over V CORPS MAIN DRESSING STATION from 21st FIELD AMBULANCE. CAPT DAVIES transferred to 47 CCS from 4 CCS. LCOM	

2449 Wt. W14957/M90 750,000 1/16 J.B.C. & A. Forms/C.2118/12.

Army Form C. 2118.

Instructions regarding War Diaries and Intelligence Summaries are contained in F. S. Regs., Part II. and the Staff Manual respectively. Title Pages will be prepared in manuscript.

WAR DIARY
or
~~INTELLIGENCE~~ SUMMARY
(Erase heading not required.)

Place	Date	Hour	Summary of Events and Information	Remarks and references to Appendices
ACHEUX.	12 4 17		DRESSING STATION at FORCEVILLE taken over – all medical stores etc to be brought to ACHEUX. SCABIES dept of Hospital at ACHEUX in running order – [initials]	
"	17 4 17		2/2 HOME COUNTIES FIELD AMBULANCE evacuated ~~[illegible]~~ patients to this hospital. [initials]	
"	18 4 17		DDMS V CORPS visited Hospital	
"	20 4 17		LT MAILE detailed to attend sick at No 66 P of W Camp BERTRANCOURT [initials]	
"	22 4 17		CAPT MALKIN struck off strength of unit. C.O. & CAPT CUMMINGS attended lecture at ACHIET LE GRAND. LIEUT MAILE detailed to attend sick at NOS 15 – 37 – 46 P. of W Camps at AUTHIE – BUS-LES-ARTOIS & THIEVRES. [initials]	
"	24 4 17	8 pm	CAPT MATHEWS rejoined unit. [initials]	
"	24 4 17	3 pm	D.D.M.S. V Corps visited Hospital.	

[signature]
D.C. ... HOME COUNTIES
FIELD AMBULANCE R.A.M.C.

Medical

58th Div.

140/2161.

Vol 4

May 1917

5

CONFIDENTIAL
****

W A R   D I A R Y

OF

2/3rd H.C. Fd Amb

From 1/5/17

To 26/5/17

Instructions regarding War Diaries and Intelligence Summaries are contained in F. S. Regs., Part II. and the Staff Manual respectively. Title Pages will be prepared in manuscript.

WAR DIARY
or
~~INTELLIGENCE SUMMARY~~

(Erase heading not required.)

2/3RD HOME COUNTIES FIELD AMBULANCE.
No. ....
Date ....

Army Form C. 2118.

Place	Date	Hour	Summary of Events and Information	Remarks and references to Appendices
ACHEUX	1-5-17		Daily state – Remaining in hospital 127 – admitted 3 – discharged 11 – To CCS 8	LCDM
"	2-5-17		Daily state – Remaining in hospital 109 – " 4 – " 21 – " 6	
			CAPT. MALKIN took over medical charge of 2/12th LONDON REGt. – CAPT. HAYES SMITH reported for duty –	LCDM
"	3-5-17		Daily state Remaining in hospital 108 – admitted 7 – discharged 6 – To CCS 3	LCDM
		11 AM.	Notice received from A.D.M.S to be ready to move at 3 hours notice –	
"	4-5-17	7 AM	Orders received from A.D.M.S for one Section to proceed to ACHIET-LE-GRAND & camp near the 2/2nd H.C.F.A.	
		9.30 AM	– Section proceeded & reached destination at 7.30 PM –	
			Daily state. Remaining in hospital 95 – admitted 2 – discharged 13 – To CCS 2.	LCDM
		12 Midnight	Major Fulton proceeded to England on leave –	
"	5.5.17		Daily state – Remaining in Hospital 74 – admitted nil – Discharged 15 – To CCS 6.	LCDM
"	6.5.17		Daily state Remaining " 68 – " 5 – " 6 – " 5	LCDM
"	7.5.17		Daily state " " 65 – " 3 – " 6	LCDM
"	8.5.17		Daily state " " 56 – " 3 – " 6 – " 6	LCDM
"	9.5.17		Daily state " " 48 – " 1 – " 7 – " 2	LCDM
"	10.5.17		Daily state " " 39 – " nil – " 5 – " 4	LCDM
"	11.5.17	7.10 AM	Orders from ADMS to move Field Amb: to site at ACHIET-LE-GRAND – leaving one tent subdivision to hand over hospital & one tent subdivision at No 4 CCS VARENNES.	
		10.30 AM	Field Amb: moved & arrived at destination at 7.20 PM	
		9. AM.	2/2 Fd Amb: Hospital taken over	LCDM.

Army Form C. 2118.

Inst[illegible]ions regarding War Diaries and Intelligence [illegible]mmaries are contained in F. S. Regs., Part II. [illegible]nd the Staff Manual respectively. Title Pages will be prepared in manuscript.

WAR DIARY

or

~~INTELLIGENCE SUMMARY~~

(Erase heading not required.)

Place	Date	Hour	Summary of Events and Information	Remarks and references to Appendices
ACHEUX.	11.5.17		Daily state. Remaining in hospital - 36 - admitted 3 - Discharged 4 - To CCS 2. [illegible]	
ACHEUX	12.5.17		Daily state " " 36 - —— nil —— nil —— nil [illegible]	
ACHIET-LE-GRAND		9.15 PM	Tent subdivision from ACHEUX arrived, having been relieved by 2/2 WEST RIDING FLD. AMB. - 26 Patients handed over to this Ambulance. [illegible]	
" "	13.5.17		Daily state - Remaining in hospital 135 - admitted 98 - Discharged 15 - To C.C.S 15. [illegible]	
" "	14.5.17		Daily state - " " 121 - " 13 - " 27 - —— nil	
		7.30 PM	one Section of Fld Amb. proceeded to take over site of Fld Amb at BEHAGNIES. [illegible]	
"	15.5.17		Handed over hospital & 149 patients to 22nd Fld Amb.	
		9.50 AM	Main body of Fld Amb proceeded to BEHAGNIES & arrived at 11.45 AM.	
BEHAGNIES.		5 PM	order from ADMS. to have 3 officers & 100 bearers ready to proceed to 2/2nd H.C FA. at ½ hours notice [illegible]	
BEHAGNIES	17.5.17		Daily state Remaining in hospital 28 - admitted 39 - discharged nil - To C.C.S 12 -	
		10.30 PM	Orders from A.D.M.S. for 3 officers & 100 bearers to proceed up the line -	
		11 PM	Party moved. [illegible]	
		12 PM.	Major FULTON returned from leave -	
" "	18.5.17	9 AM	C.O. proceeded to MORY to take command of 2/2 H.C.F.A.	
		9 PM	one officer & 96 bearers returned to BEHAGNIES after evacuating wounded from BULLECOURT.	
			Casualties - CAPT. W. G. CUMMINGS - killed in action - one man died of wounds (4472nd Pte Allison A) - 4 other ranks wounded -	
		9 PM.	Major FULTON left to take command of 2/2nd H.C.F.A. [illegible]	
			Daily state Remaining in hospital - 57 - admitted 32 - To C.C.S 5	

Instructions regarding War Diaries and Intelligence Summaries are contained in F. S. Regs., Part II. and the Staff Manual respectively. Title Pages will be prepared in manuscript.

WAR DIARY
or
~~INTELLIGENCE SUMMARY~~
(Erase heading not required.)

Army Form C. 2118.

Place	Date	Hour	Summary of Events and Information	Remarks and references to Appendices
BEHAGNIES.	19/5/17		Daily state – Remaining in hospital – 86 – admitted 58 – Discharged 3 – To CCS 31	
		6 PM.	FUNERAL of the Late CAPT. W.G. CUMMINGS at MORY.	
		7.30 PM	C.O. rejoined unit.	[initials]
	20/5/17		Daily state – Remaining in Hospital 57 – admitted 43 – Discharged 5. To CCS. 47 – To C.R.S 20.	
		8 AM	Letter from ADMS congratulating unit on efficient manner in which wounded were evacuated from BULLECOURT on 18-5-17 –	
		10 PM.	operation order No 22 received from ADMS. re sending some more bearers up the line –	[initials]
	21/5/17		Daily state Remaining in hospital 56 – admitted 44 – Discharged 10. To CCS 24 To CRS 11	
		3 AM.	one officer & 36 men proceeded to DURNO'S POST to report to O.C. 2/2 HCFA for duty –	
		6 PM.	one officer & 48 other ranks proceeded to DURNO'S POST to relieve previous party	
		12 midday	CAPT: GERATY. L – & CAPT FERGUSON. P. reported for duty –	
		6 PM.	CAPT GERATY – ordered to report to O.C. 2/2 HCFA for permanent duty –	
		11.30 PM	ADMS visited Hospital.	[initials]
	22/5/17		Daily state Remaining in Hospital – 47 – admitted 32 – Discharged 5 – To CCS 16 – To CRS 20.	
			The following letter received from A.D.M.S. — "The ADMS 58th Div: has noted	

2149 Wt. W14957/M90 750,000 1/16 J.B.C. & A. Forms/C.2118/12.

Army Form C. 2118.

Instructions regarding War Diaries and Intelligence Summaries are contained in F. S. Regs., Part II. and the Staff Manual respectively. Title Pages will be prepared in manuscript.

WAR DIARY
or
~~INTELLIGENCE~~ SUMMARY
(Erase heading not required.)

Place	Date	Hour	Summary of Events and Information	Remarks and references to Appendices
			with much appreciation the efficient manner in which the wounded were cleared from BULLECOURT on 18-5-17 - by the 2/3rd Home Counties Field Amb: - Please convey to Capt. W.C.D Moir RAMC.T & N.C.O.s & men of the bearer division, the congratulations of the ADMS on the manner in which this difficult task has been accomplished." -	
			The following have been mentioned for good work - [illegible] 497020 Sgt Richardson. W. 497264 L.Cpl Stenning H.T 497314 Pte Croft. V. WCDM	
BEHAGNIES	23/5/17		Daily state Remaining in hospital - 48 - admitted 21 - To C.C.S 11 - To duty - 1 - To C.R.S 8.	
			497404 Pte Skinner, R Killed in action - WCDM	
"	24/5/17		Daily state Remaining in hospital 46 - admitted - 37 - To C.C.S 14 - To C.R.S - 17. To duty 8 -	
			Capt. Ferguson ordered to report to O.C. 45 C.C.S for duty - WCDM	
"	25/5/17		Daily state Remaining in hospital 36 - admitted 27 - To C.C.S 16 - To C.R.S. 21.	
			C.O. proceeded to inspect the line of evacuation of wounded to M.D.S. ERVILLERS. WCDM	
		11 PM	Hostile aircraft over camp -	
"	26/5/17	9.15AM	C.O. visited A.D.M.S.	

J Barkley
LIEUT. COL.
O.C. 2nd/3rd HOME COUNTIES
FIELD AMBULANCE R.A.M.C.
WCDM.

26/5/17

2149 Wt. W14957/M90 750,000 1/16 J.B.C. & A. Forms/C.2118/12.

1917

140/2230

2/3rd Home Counties F.A.

Instructions regarding War Diaries and Intelligence Summaries are contained in F. S. Regs., Part II. and the Staff Manual respectively. Title Pages will be prepared in manuscript.

7

WAR DIARY
or
~~INTELLIGENCE SUMMARY~~

(Erase heading not required.)

2/3RD HOME COUNTIES FIELD AMBULANCE.
No.........
Date.........

Vol

Army Form C. 2118.

Place	Date	Hour	Summary of Events and Information	Remarks and references to Appendices
ERVILLERS	1.6.17		Daily State. Remaining - 18, admitted - 49, to CCS 12, to CRS 15.	Ewm
		7pm	Warning order - If wind favourable a gas cloud would be launched.	Ewm
"	2.6.17		Daily state Remaining. 40, admitted - 44, to CCS 10, to CRS - 15, discharged to duty. 1	Ewm
		3am	Order that gas attack would NOT take place	Ewm
		7pm	Warning order - If wind favourable a gas attack would be launched - If the attack was to take place the code word 'Goosebury' would be used and if NOT 'Rhubarb'.	Ewm
		12 midnight	Message received reading 'Goosebury'.	Ewm
"	3.6.17		Daily State Remaining - 58, admitted - 47, to CCS 12, to CRS 49, discharged to duty 9.	Ewm
			Lt + QM. F. POOLE proceeded on 10 days leave to England.	Ewm
"	4.6.17		Daily State Remaining - 45, admitted - 28, to CCS 3, to CRS 22.	Ewm
"	5.6.17		Daily State Remaining - 38, admitted - 29, to CCS 15, to CRS 21 discharged to duty 1.	Ewm
"	6.6.17		Daily State Remaining - 30, admitted - 55, to CCS 13, to CRS 18 discharged to duty 1.	Ewm
"	7.6.17		Daily State Remaining - 53, admitted - 32, to CCS 5, to CRS 21 discharged to duty 1.	Ewm
"	8.6.17		Daily State Remaining - 58, admitted - 78, to CCS 28, to CRS 23 discharged to duty 7	Ewm
"	9.6.17		Daily State Remaining - 78, admitted - 41, to CCS 13, to CRS 44, discharged to duty 5.	Ewm
			C.O. proceeded to CROISSILLES and inspected the Routes of Evacuation for wounded.	Ewm
"	10.6.17		Daily State Remaining 57, admitted 46, to CCS 16, to CRS 30, discharged to duty 6	Ewm
"	11.6.17		Daily State Remaining 51, admitted 41, to CCS 33, to CRS 49, discharged to duty 7	Ewm
"	12.6.17		Daily State Remaining 3, admitted 53, to CCS 8, to CRS 21 discharged to duty 1	Ewm
"	13.6.17		Daily State Remaining 20, admitted 47, to CCS 10, to CRS 30 discharged to duty 2.	Ewm
"	14.6.17		Daily State Remaining 17, admitted 43, to CCS 21, to CRS 28, discharged to duty 5	Ewm
			TWO OFFICERS & 105 other ranks detailed to A.D.S. ST LEGER. C.O. proceeded to R.A.P. to supervise the Evacuation of wounded	Ewm

2449 Wt. W14957/M90 750,000 1/16 J.B.C. & A. Forms/C.2118/12.

Instructions regarding War Diaries and Intelligence Summaries are contained in F. S. Regs., Part II. and the Staff Manual respectively. Title Pages will be prepared in manuscript.

WAR DIARY
or
~~INTELLIGENCE SUMMARY~~
(Erase heading not required.)

Army Form C. 2118.

Place	Date	Hour	Summary of Events and Information	Remarks and references to Appendices
ERVILLERS	14.6.17		Lt & Q.M. F. POOLE returned from 10 days leave in ENGLAND.	Ewm
"	15.6.17		Daily State Remaining 6, admitted 45, to CCS 13, to CRS 31, to duty 4	Ewm
			37 stretcher bearers of 2/1st H.C. FIELD AMB reported for duty at A.D.S. ST LEGER.	Ewm
		9pm	18 N.C.O. & 9 men reported as reinforcements.	Ewm
"	16.6.17		Daily State Remaining 3, admitted 33, to CCS 5, to CRS 18, to duty 3	Ewm
			37 stretcher bearers of 2/1st H.C. FIELD AMB. reported for duty at A.D.S. ST. LEGER.	Ewm
"	17.6.17		Daily State Remaining 10, admitted 41, to CCS 8, to CRS 25, to duty 17	Ewm
"		5pm	C.O. and 40 other ranks returned to ERVILLERS from A.D.S. – MAJOR Herbert Dixon attached to 2/3 H.C.F.A. for duty	Ewm
"	18.6.17		Daily State Remaining 11, admitted 47, to CCS 15, to CRS 24, to duty 2.	Ewm
"	19.6.17		Daily State Remaining 17, admitted 75, to CCS 25, to CRS 32, to duty 11. Major HERBERT DIXON rejoined to 2/2 H.C.F.A.	Ewm
"	20.6.17		Daily State Remaining 24, admitted 45, to CCS 22, to CRS 28, to duty 6	Ewm
			CAPT W.C.D. MAILE recalled from A.D.S. St LEGER.	Ewm
"	21.6.17		Daily State Remaining 13, admitted 45, to CCS 12, to CRS 29, to duty 3.	Ewm
"	22.6.17		Daily State Remaining 14, admitted 37, to CCS 11, to CRS 27, to duty 6	Ewm
			CAPT W.C.D. MAILE proceeded on 10 days leave to ENGLAND	Ewm
		9pm	Operation Order to move FIELD AMBULANCE to BUCQUOY on 23rd inst.	Ewm
"	23.6.17		Daily State Remaining 7, admitted 34, to CCS 11, to CRS 29, to 22nd FIELD AMB. 1	Ewm
		10.30am	FIELD AMBULANCE moved off from ERVILLERS	Ewm
		2.20pm	FIELD AMBULANCE arrived BUCQUOY.	Ewm
		9.30pm	Details from A.D.S. ST LEGER arrived BUCQUOY	Ewm
BUCQUOY	24.6.17		NIL	Ewm
	25.6.17		Lt Col J. BARKLEY to act as A.D.M.S. during Col HOUGHTON's absence.	Ewm

2149 Wt. W14957/M90 750,000 1/16 J.B.C. & A. Forms/C.2118/12.

Army Form C. 2118.

Instructions regarding War Diaries and Intelligence Summaries are contained in F. S. Regs., Part II. and the Staff Manual respectively. Title Pages will be prepared in manuscript.

WAR DIARY
or
~~INTELLIGENCE SUMMARY~~
(Erase heading not required.)

Place	Date	Hour	Summary of Events and Information	Remarks and references to Appendices
BOCQUOY	26.6.17		Inoculated cases of 2/1st LONDON REGT and own Unit being admitted for 24 hours, ~~and~~ and on subsequent days.	Ewm
"	27.6.17	9am	MAJOR H. DIXON arrived to take command of the Unit during Lt Col BARKLEY'S absence on leave	Ewm
"	28.6.17	11.30am	D.D.M.S. 5th CORPS inspected the Camp.	Ewm
		7.30pm	CAPT. H.G. MASSY-MILES reported for duty with this Unit.	Ewm
"	29.6.17	7pm	Order from DDMS. V. Corps reading. "58th Division - 2/3rd H.C. Field Ambulance at Bucquoy Dental Surgeon from No 45 CCS at 9.30 a.m. on Tuesdays & Fridays	Ewm
"	30.6.17	5.5am	497339 Pte TAYLOR. W.H. of 2/3rd H.C. Field Ambulance was found lying dead whilst on picquet.	Ewm

30/6/17

Herbert Dixon
Major RAMC T
OC 2nd/3rd HOME COUNTIES FIELD AMBULANCE R.A.M.C.

2449 Wt. W14957/M90 750,000 1/16 J.B.C. & A. Forms/C.2118/12.

6

July 917

140/2298

Medical

Vol 6

WAR DIARY

2/3rd H. C. Field Ambulance

July 1917

Instructions regarding War Diaries and Intelligence Summaries are contained in F. S. Regs., Part II. and the Staff Manual respectively. Title Pages will be prepared in manuscript.

WAR DIARY
or
~~INTELLIGENCE SUMMARY~~
(Erase heading not required.)

2/3RD HOME COUNTIES FIELD AMBULANCE.
No. ....
Date ....

Army Form C. 2118.

Place	Date	Hour	Summary of Events and Information	Remarks and references to Appendices
BUCQUOY	1/7/17		Post mortem on Pte TAYLOR W.H	WWM.
"	2/7/17		Burial of Pte TAYLOR W.H. CAPT. S. DAVIES evacuated sick to Base	WWM.
	3/7/17		MAJOR H. DIXON to new area	WWM.
"	5/7/17		CAPT. MATTHEWS + C Section to ADS. METZ + to take over FA site at NEUVILLE	WWM
	6/7/17		Main body to BANCOURT with 174th Bde left 3 PM + arrive 8.30 pm	
	7/7/17		MAJOR H. DIXON + A.D.M.S. visit to line. Main body to BUS at 1.30 pm arrive 4.30 pm +	WWM.
BUS	7/7/17		CAPT. W.W. MAXWELL + Party returned from No 45 C.C.S. MAJOR H. DIXON visit to line 8.45 pm	
		4.30 pm	Corps Main Dressing Station taken over — Horses commenced stampeding 8.30 pm. 21 still missing. Severe Thunderstorm mid night + early morning 7/7/17 – 8/7/17	
	8/7/17		Sun O/C. M.A.C. Sun O/C F.A. 1/3 E. Lancs. Surgeon Gen. MACPHERSON DDGMS called. ADMS 58th Div called	WWM
	9/7/17		C Section to 2/1 H C F.A. from 10/7/17 also 2 Sick Wagons + 1 FORD Car. 10 a.m CAPT. H.G. MASEY-MILES to 2/8 Lond Regt. for duty in place of CAPT. GAWN evacuated Sick. CAPT. G.M. MACGILLIVRAY + CAPT. GOURLAY + C Section of 2/2 H.C.F.A arrived for duty here 9 pm	WWM
	10/7/17	11 a.m	A.D.M.S. 58th Lond Div. visited Camp + Wards. 3 pm D.A.D.M.S. 58th LOND Div called	WWM
"	11/7/17		Lt Col J. BARKLEY returned from leave	WWM
"	15/7/17		LIEUT. T.P. EDMUNDSON U.S ARMY reported for duty —	WWM
"	17/7/17		CAPT. GOURLAY + 10 other ranks proceeded to 29 C.C.S for duty —	WWM
				WWM

2449 Wt. W14957/M90 750,000 1/16 J.B.C. & A. Forms/C.2118/12.

Army Form C. 2118.

Instructions regarding War Diaries and Intelligence Summaries are contained in F. S. Regs., Part II. and the Staff Manual respectively. Title Pages will be prepared in manuscript.

WAR DIARY
~~or~~
~~INTELLIGENCE SUMMARY~~

(Erase heading not required.)

Place	Date	Hour	Summary of Events and Information	Remarks and references to Appendices
BUS	17/7/17 (contd)		LIEUT: DISHINGTON. 2/2 H.C.F.A reported for duty – [illegible]	
"	19/7/17		CAPT. McGILLIVARY + 34 other ranks of 2/2 H.C.F.A returned to their unit – [illegible]	
"	21/7/17		497485 Pte LINDSEY. E.F.W. proceeded to England for commission in the Infantry – [illegible] LIEUT. DISHINGTON ~~rejoined~~ left for duty at 2/1st H.C.F.A. D.D.M.S. IV CORPS visited camp – [illegible]	
"	23/7/17		operation order No 25 received re move to FOSSEUX Area – [illegible]	
"	25/7/17		G.O.C. IV CORPS & DDMS & ADMS. visited camp – [illegible]	
"	26/7/17		CAPT. W.C.D. MAILE & 10 other ranks proceeded as an advance party to WANQUENTIN. C.O. visited WANQUENTIN & returned to BUS.	
"	27/7/17		LIEUT: DISHINGTON reported for duty. [illegible]	
"	28/7/17		All horse transport less 2 limbers & 1 ambulance wagon under command of CAPT. HAYES SMITH proceeded with 174 Brigade transport by road to WANQUENTIN – [illegible]	
"	29/7/17		497327 Pte. HORSFIELD. R. proceeded to England for a commission in Infantry [illegible]	
		1.30 PM	Main body by road to BAPAUME – thence by rail to SAULTY – thence by road to WANQUENTIN – arriving at destination about 1.30 AM.	
WANQUENTIN	30/7/17	5.30 AM	Move completed – 1 ambulance wagon left BUS with 173 Brigade to new area – [illegible]	
"	31/7/17	11 AM	Ambulance wagon arrived. LIEUT. DISHINGTON rejoined his unit – [illegible]	[signature] LIEUT. COL. O.C. 2nd/3rd HOME COUNTIES FIELD AMBULANCE R.A.M.C.

Confidential

4

Aug. 1917

5

Medical

Vol-7

140/2364

War Diary

of

2/3rd H.C. Field Ambulance

For the month of August 1917

B.E.F.

SUMMARY OF MEDICAL WAR DIARIES OF 2/3rd H.C.F.A. 58th Div.

18th Corps. 5th ARMY.

Western Front Operations - Aug.-Sept. 1917.

Officer Commanding - Lt.Col. J. Barkley.

SUMMARISED UNDER THE FOLLOWING HEADINGS :-

Phase "D" 1. Passchendaele Operations,"July - Nov. 1917."

(a) - Operations commencing July 31st 1917.

Instructions regarding War Diaries and Intelligence Summaries are contained in F. S. Regs., Part II. and the Staff Manual respectively. Title Pages will be prepared in manuscript.

WAR DIARY
or
~~INTELLIGENCE SUMMARY~~
(Erase heading not required.)

Army Form C. 2118.

2/3RD HOME COUNTIES FIELD AMBULANCE

Place	Date	Hour	Summary of Events and Information	Remarks and references to Appendices
WANQUETIN	Aug		Field Ambulance encamped at WANQUETIN in SIMENCOURT Rd receiving sick from 174th + 175 I Brigades. These sick were evacuated 1st when received — to duty — 2nd if the illness persisted for more than three days to 2/1 HC Amb at AVESNES LES COMPTES and 3rd for longer illnesses to CCS.	JM
WANQUETIN	5th		Cases not discharged to duty are now all evacuated to AVESNES LES COMPTES for transmission to CCS if necessary.	JM
WANQUETIN	11th		Arranged spray baths for the men + patients. Numbers of latter to be kept up to 100.	
			CAPT JAMIESON + LT. BEAUMONT attached to Field Ambulance	JM
	16		Troops drilling in small square behind canteen. Portuguese Railway troops arrived and occupied a great part of the encampment near Field Ambulance	JM
	22		Preparing to move, all patients discharged or sent to Avesnes LES COMPTES. Practically all C Section equipment medical, surgical + ordnance handed in giving much needed relief to transport	JM

[signature]
LIEUT. COL.
O.C. 2ND/3RD HOME COUNTIES
FIELD AMBULANCE R.A.M.C.

2449 Wt. W14957/M90 750,000 1/16 J.B.C. & A. Forms/C.2118/12.

Instructions regarding War Diaries and Intelligence Summaries are contained in F. S. Regs., Part II. and the Staff Manual respectively. Title Pages will be prepared in manuscript.

WAR DIARY
or
~~INTELLIGENCE~~ SUMMARY
(Erase heading not required.)

Army Form C. 2118.

2/3RD HOME COUNTIES FIELD AMBULANCE.
No. ....
Date ....

Place	Date	Hour	Summary of Events and Information	Remarks and references to Appendices
WANQUETIN	Aug 23.		LIEUT MAILE and three other ranks proceeded as advanced party to our new area near POPERINGHE.	MB
L'EBBE FARM POPERINGHE	25		Main body entrained at AUBIGNY and proceeded to POPERINGHE arriving there at 5.30pm. Move completed at 7.15 pm.	MB
L'EBBE FARM.	26		C.O., Major DIXON & CAPT. MAILE proceeded via ELVERDIGNE to DUHALLOW A.D.S. Sheet 28. C25 d 3.0 thence to LA BELLE ALLIANCE (Sheet 28 C20.a 6.5.), Divl collecting post from which they proceeded to walk over routes of evacuation. CO proceeded with ADMS to TIN HUT Sheet 28. C.23 a 4.2. There are an enormous number of guns around and the ground + roads very much cut up. Returned to Hdqtrs at 8.30pm.	MB
do	27		Received Operation Order No 26. ADMS Capt. JAMIESON & LIEUT BEAUMONT visited Adv Divl. Collecting Post C 22 b 5.1 Sheet 28 where they had to remain, owing to heavy shelling, for some time.	MB
	28.		visited C 20 a 6 5 (Sheet 28) Rear Divl. Collecting Post and discussed method of evacuation with O/c Post.	MB
DUHALLOW ADS In the line.	29	11 am	Took over Advanced Posts East of YSER CANAL from 1/2 S.M. Fd Amb. Remainder of Fd Amb + transport moved to GWENT FARM. A 28. a 5.5. Sheet 28. Bearer divisions allotted posts in line of evacuation under Major DIXON with CAPT JAMIESON & LT BEAUMONT. Hdqtrs of 2/3 H.C. Fd Amb opened at A.D.S. DUHALLOW.	MB
		10pm	1 Corpl attached killed (Cpl MARTIN} 1/2nd S.M. Fd Amb) Pte W.W. GAY 2/3 H.C. F.A. killed 1 N.C.O. wounded. Rear Divl Collecting Post shelled, one 4.9 (?) blew in the end of a dug out.	MB

2449 Wt. W14957/M90 750,000 1/16 J.B.C. & A. Forms/C.2118/12.

Instructions regarding War Diaries and Intelligence Summaries are contained in F. S. Regs., Part II. and the Staff Manual respectively. Title Pages will be prepared in manuscript.

WAR DIARY
or
INTELLIGENCE SUMMARY
(Erase heading not required.)

2/3RD HOME COUNTIES FIELD AMBULANCE
No. ....
Date ....

Army Form C. 2118.

Place	Date	Hour	Summary of Events and Information	Remarks and references to Appendices
In the line	30	5 am	Proceeded up the routes of evacuation, inspected and visited all posts. All very dirty and wet. Ordered general cleaning up and put out directing signs as far as possible. There is a great deal of work to be done in improving and sandbagging various shelters. In afternoon A.D.M.S. visit posts.	[initials]
do	31		Went up the line at 9 am. Met A.D.M.S. and AA + Q.M.G. 58th Divn. accompanied them to ADMIRALS RD. and A.D.M.S. selected site for soup kitchen at approximately C.21.a.4.5. Sheet 28.	[initials]

31/8/17

[signature]
LIEUT. COL.
O.C. 2ND/3RD HOME COUNTIES
FIELD AMBULANCE R.A.M.C.

2449 Wt. W14957/M90 750,000 1/16 J.B.C. & A. Forms/C.2118/12.

B.E.F.

2/3rd H.C.F.A. 58th Div. Western Front

18th Corps. 5th ARMY. Aug-Sept. 1917.

O .C. Lt.Col. J. Barkley.

PHASE "D" 1. - Passchendaele Operations,"July-Nov. 1917."

(a) - Operations commencing July 31st 1917.

Headquarters at L'Ebbe Farm,Poperinghe.

Aug. 25th. Moves and Transfer. Unit transferred with 58th Div. from 17th Corps III. Army to 18th Corps 5th Army and moved to L'Ebbe Farm.

29th. Moves. To A.D.S. Duhallow C.25.d.3.2.

Medical Arrangements. Adv. Posts east of Yser Canal taken over from 1/2nd S.M.F.A.

Casualties R.A.M.C. O & 2 killed. O & 1 wounded.

Sept. 2nd. Casualties R.A.M.C. Lt.Col. J. Barkley slightly wounded remained at duty.

Capt. Maile wounded.

Medical Arrangements. Bearers 2/1st H.C.F.A. relieved Bearers 2/3rd H.C.F.A. in line.

4th. Medical Arrangements. Bearers 2/2nd H.C.F.A. relieved B 2/1st H.C.F.A. in line.

6th. Casualties R.A.M.C. 0 & 2 wounded.

7th. Casualties R.A.M.C., Gas. 0 & 3 2/2nd H.C.F.A. gassed.

8th. Casualties R.A.M.C. 0 & 1 wounded.

9th. 0 & 1 wounded.

11th. 0 & 1 wounded.

15th. Medical Arrangements. Bearers 2/3rd H.C.F.A. relieved Bearers 2/2nd H.C.F.A. in line.

Casualties R.A.M.C. 0 & 1 wounded.

6

Instructions regarding War Diaries and Intelligence Summaries are contained in F. S. Regs., Part II. and the Staff Manual respectively. Title Pages will be prepared in manuscript.

WAR DIARY
or
INTELLIGENCE SUMMARY
(Erase heading not required.)

2/3RD HOME COUNTIES FIELD AMBULANCE. No. .... Date ....

Army Form C. 2118.

Vol 8

M95
948

Place	Date	Hour	Summary of Events and Information	Remarks and references to Appendices
			WAR DIARY - MEDICAL - FOR MONTH OF SEPTEMBER of 2/3rd HOME COUNTIES FIELD AMBULANCE. R.A.M.C. H H Leeson Capt. LIEUT. COL. O.C. 2ND/3RD HOME COUNTIES FIELD AMBULANCE R.A.M.C.	

2449 Wt. W14957/M90 750,000 1/16 J.B.C. & A. Forms/C.2118/12.

Instructions regarding War Diaries and Intelligence Summaries are contained in F. S. Regs., Part II. and the Staff Manual respectively. Title Pages will be prepared in manuscript.

WAR DIARY
or
~~INTELLIGENCE SUMMARY~~
(Erase heading not required.)

2/3RD HOME COUNTIES FIELD AMBULANCE.
No.........
Date.........

Army Form C. 2118.

Place	Date	Hour	Summary of Events and Information	Remarks and references to Appendices
Sheet 28. C. 25. d. 3 0.	1-9.17	9 am.	C.O visited forward area.	
		11 am	A.D.M.S. 58th Divn at C. 25 d. 3. 0. – Bearers of 2/1st H.C. F.A. relieved bearers of 2/3rd H.C. F.A. in forward area, owing to heavy shelling in forward area on right sector, that sector was not relieved until 6 am, the remaining posts being relieved by 3 am.	
do.	2.9.17	5 am	C.O. & Capt Maile visited forward area.	
		8.45 am	C.O. slightly & Capt. Maile in right leg wounded. C.O resumed duty – Capt. Maile evacuated.	
		11 am	A.D.M.S. at C 25. d. 3 0	
		1 pm	Major Dixon reported from advanced area to C. 25. d 3 0.	
		10 am	Capt HAYES SMITH & Capt. RYAN relieved. Capt. JAMIESON & LIEUT. BEAUMONT.	
do	3.9.17		LIEUT BEAUMONT left the Unit to report to D.D.M.S. ROUEN under instruction of D.G.M.S.	
		11 am	C.O. went back to GWENT FARM.	
		4 pm	Major Dixon H. returned to C 25. d 3 0 & took charge.	
do	4.9.17	2.30 am	Relief of 2/1st H.C.F.A. by squads of 2/2 H.C.F.A. without casualties – relief was complete by 3 am.	
		6 am	Major H. DIXON visited forward area posts & returned at 11 am.	
		11 am	A.D.M.S. visited R.D.S.P & A.D.S.P.	
		6 pm	C.O. returned from GWENT FARM.	
do	5.9.17	9 am	C.O. visited all posts in forward area.	
do.	6.9.17	10 am	CAPT JAMIESON & Capt. GOURLEY relieved Capt HAYES SMITH & Capt. RYAN at R.D.C.P.	
			2 RAMC men wounded.	
do	7.9.17	5 am	C.O visited all posts in forward area.	
			Relief of squads 2/2nd H.C.F.A relieved by 2/3rd H.C.F.A	
			3 men of 2/2nd H.C.F.A. evacuated N.Y.D. Gas poisoning.	
do	8.9.17	9 am	C.O. & MAJOR H. DIXON visited forward area.	
			1 man 2/3 H.C.F.A. evacuated wounded.	
		8.0 pm	9 extra squads sent up to re-inforce the line.	

2449 Wt. W14957/M90 750,000 1/16 J.B.C. & A. Forms/C.2118/12.

Army Form C. 2118.

Instructions regarding War Diaries and Intelligence Summaries are contained in F. S. Regs., Part II. and the Staff Manual respectively. Title Pages will be prepared in manuscript.

WAR DIARY
or
~~INTELLIGENCE SUMMARY~~
(Erase heading not required.)

2/3RD HOME COUNTIES FIELD AMBULANCE
No.......
Date.......

Place	Date	Hour	Summary of Events and Information	Remarks and references to Appendices
SHEET 28	9.9.17	11 am	7 casuals rejoined Unit from line & sent to rest.	
C 25. d. 3.0.		11 am	A.D.M.S. 58th DIV. visited forward posts.	
			1 man 2/3rd H.C.F.A. wounded.	
			C.O. & CAPT. GOURLAY visited route of light railway to see if it was suitable for the evacuation of wounded from the forward area. also made inquiries as regards trucks for carrying stretchers.	
do.	10.9.17	9 am	C.O visited the Light Railway Operating Coy re evacuating by light railway	
			Capt. CAVANAGH M.O.R.C. U.S.A reported for duty Posted to R.D.C.P.	
	10.9.17	11 am	CAPT CUTHBERT reported for duty at R.D.C.P. At 11 pm. posted for duty with 2/5th LONDON REGT.	
do.	11.9.17	11 am	A.D.M.S. 58th DIV visiting forward area.	
			1 man 2/3rd H.C.F.A. wounded - returned to duty.	
do.	11.9.17		C.O visited ESSEX FARM A.D.S. re requisitioning several stretcher trucks in order to evacuate wounded.	
		10 am	LT ALTROUNYAN reported for ~~at~~ duty.	
			CAPT GOURLAY posted for duty with 2/10th LONDON REGT.	
do.	12.9.17	11 am	LT ALTROUNYAN posted for duty with 2/4th LONDON REGT.	
			CAPT. CUTHBERT reported and sent to A.D.M.S. 58th DIV for disposal.	
do.	13.9.17	noon	Capt. KENNION 2/3rd S.M.F.A. reported for duty. posted to R.D.C.P	
do.	14.9.17	noon	C.O proceeded to GWENT FARM for rest.	
			A.D.M.S. 58th DIV visiting posts.	
do.	15.9.17	11 pm	Bearer squads of 2/3rd H.C.F.A. relieved squads of 2/2nd H.C.F.A in line. 1 man 2/3rd H.C.F.A wounded.	
do.	16.9.17	3.15 am	CAPT BELL M.O i/c 2/3rd LONDON REGT. killed in action. 2 men 2/3rd H.C.F.A. wounded.	
		11 am	A.D.M.S. 58th DIV. visiting forward area	
do.	17.9.17		C.O returned from rest.	
do.	18.9.17		C.O. & A.D.M.S 58th DIV. inspecting all routes of evacuation of casualties.	
do.	19.9.17		3 large cars reported for duty in forward area.	

Instructions regarding War Diaries and Intelligence Summaries are contained in F. S. Regs., Part II. and the Staff Manual respectively. Title Pages will be prepared in manuscript.

WAR DIARY
or
~~INTELLIGENCE SUMMARY~~
(Erase heading not required.)

2/3RD HOME COUNTIES FIELD AMBULANCE
No. ....
Date ....

Army Form C. 2118.

Place	Date	Hour	Summary of Events and Information	Remarks and references to Appendices
SHEET 28. C. 25 a. 3. 0	19.9.17	6.30pm	All R.A.M.C. bearers on routes of evacuation relieved by men of 2/9 LONDON REGT. – 3 Officers 176 N.C.O's and men. CAPT. GRIFFITHS in charge.	
do.	20.9.17	8 am.	CAPT. L. HADEN. GUEST. reported at ADSP. CALIFORNIA for duty.	
		6.30am	C.O. to ADSP and then to advanced posts.	
		4 pm	D.D.M.S. XVIII Corps visited C. 25. a. 3. 0	
		6 pm.	80 R.A.M.C. bearers sent to forward area to collect any cases lying out.	
			497216 Sgt. SMITH A.G. 2/3 H.C.F.A. captured 2 GERMAN MEDICAL OFFICERS from vicinity about C. 11. c. 9. 8.	
do.	21.9.17.	2 pm	80 R.A.M.C. bearers to forward area searching captured ground for wounded.	
		3 pm	G.O.C. FIFTH ARMY at C. 25. a. 3. 0.	
			Ford Ambulances able to run up to ST. JULIEN R.A.P. at C. 18. a. 1. 8.	
			Quantity of medical stores captured at HUBNER FARM D. 1. B. 4. 8 – used as a GERMAN DRESSING POST – removed to C. 25. a. 3. 0.	
do.	22.9.17	noon	All bearers (R.A.M.C. and R.S.B's) withdrawn from line. Posts on route of evacuation manned by ordinary number of R.A.M.C. men.	
			Posts at R.D.L.P. & Cross roads closed & all equipment transferred to A.D.C.P. CALIFORNIA.	
			FORD CAR. No. 25654 destroyed by shell fire at C. 18 a. 1. 8. Chassis salved.	
do.	23.9.17	11 am.	MAJOR H. DIXON sent to take charge of XVIII C.W.W.C.P.	
		11 am	CAPT. GAWN & CAPT. LEESON reported for duty.	
do	24.9.17	noon.	LT. CAVANAGH. M.O.R.C. U.S.A. & 19 other ranks reported for temporary duty at 4 C.C.S.	
do.	24.9.17	3 pm	A.D.C.P. CALIFORNIA heavily shelled.	
		5 pm	3 Ford Cars destroyed, chassis of one salved also engine of another. Canvas of 2 large Ambulances badly damaged. Kitchen blown up, also part of dressing room. Casualties. 5 M.T. A.S.C. men, 2 returned to duty, 4 R.A.M.C. men. wounded.	
do.	25.9.17	6 am	C.O. inspected routes of evacuation.	
		11 am	CAPT. GAWN posted for duty with 291st Bde. R.F.A.	
			3 Ford Ambulances 48 Div reported for duty.	

(A49) Wt. W14957/M90 750,000 1/16 J.B.C. & A. Forms/C.2118/12.

Instructions regarding War Diaries and Intelligence Summaries are contained in F. S. Regs., Part II. and the Staff Manual respectively. Title Pages will be prepared in manuscript.

WAR DIARY
or
~~INTELLIGENCE SUMMARY~~
(Erase heading not required.)

2/3RD HOME COUNTIES FIELD AMBULANCE.

Army Form C. 2118.

Place	Date	Hour	Summary of Events and Information	Remarks and references to Appendices
SHEET 28 C.25 d 3 0	25.9.17	9 pm.	72 R.A.M.C. stretcher bearers sent up to reinforce line.	
			CAPT. LEESON posted as O/C Bearers in Forward Area.	
			1 Ford Ambulance damaged by shell fire repairable.	
		8 pm	A.D.C.P. heavily shelled. 1 M.T. A.S.C. man wounded, also 1 R.A.M.C. man.	
do.	26-9-17	5 am	C.O. to forward area. Lt POOLE to duty at A.D.C.P.	
		10 am	6 horse Ambulances sent to evacuate wounded from A.D.C.P. Returned at 2 pm.	
			3 men 2/3rd H.C.F.A. wounded. 497535 Pte CURD. J.L. killed	
		10 am	A.D.C.P. being heavily shelled	
			40 Bearers sent to forward area (JANET FARM) & 40 at C.25.d.3.0. in reserve.	
			Road from A.D.S. to A.D.C.P. CALIFORNIA impassable owing to damage done by shelling.	
		9.15 am	Road reopened.	
		11 am	CAPT. LEESON reported difficulty in dealing with wounded & asking for more bearers. 5 squads sent forward.	
		6 pm	Operation Order No 27. A.D.M.S. 58th DIVN & Administrative instructions from H.Q. 58 DIVN received, regarding 58th Divn being relieved by 48th DIV & proceeding to a back area.	
do.		10 pm	Report received that more men (stretcher bearers) were required in the forward area. 10 squads sent up.	
	27-9-17	6 am	4 squads R.A.M.C. bearers sent to forward area.	
		10 am	Capt F ELLIOTT detailed to report No 4 C.C.S. for temporary duty by noon.	
		9 am	47 stretcher cases & 54 walking wounded passed through A.D.C.P. CALIFORNIA between 9 pm 26/9/17 & 9 am 27/9/17	
		7 pm	3 Ford Ambulances of 18th DIV returned. 2 to Lt Col W.M.B. SPARKES. D.S.O. R.A.M.C. at TSW(?) FARM & 1 to XVIII C.M.O.S.	
		7 pm	173 I Bde No. 45 received re move to new area.	
do.	28.9.17	3 am	28 squads of bearers from forward area sent to rest at GWENT FARM.	

2449 Wt. W14957/M90 750,000 1/16 J.B.C. & A. Forms/C.2118/12.

Army Form C. 2118.

Instructions regarding War Diaries and Intelligence Summaries are contained in F. S. Regs., Part II. and the Staff Manual respectively. Title Pages will be prepared in manuscript.

WAR DIARY
or
~~INTELLIGENCE SUMMARY~~
(Erase heading not required.)

2/3RD HOME COUNTIES FIELD AMBULANCE
No. ....
Date ....

Place	Date	Hour	Summary of Events and Information	Remarks and references to Appendices
Sheet 28. C.25.d.2.0.	28.9.17	2.30pm	A.D.C.P. CALIFORNIA heavily shelled.	
		3.30am	All personnel of Field Ambulance of 58th DIV relieved by personnel of 1/3rd S.M.F.A. All relieved personnel to GWENT FARM.	
GWENT FARM SHEET 28 A.28.a.5.5.	28.9.17	7pm	Bearers of 2/1st & 2/2nd H.C. F.A's despatched to their respective Units.	
	29.9.17	11am	C.O., LT. POOLE & 5 other ranks proceeded by Ambulance car to BLANC PIGNON as advanced party, also all motor transport.	
do.	30.9.17	12.15am	Transport section less 2 limbered G.S wagons joined 175th I. Bde Transport convoy at junction of POPERINGHE – ELVERDINGHE road and the VLAMERTINGHE SWITCH road.	

J H Wheeson Capt.
for LIEUT. COL.
O.C. 2ND/3RD HOME COUNTIES
FIELD AMBULANCE R.A.M.C.

2449 Wt. W14957/M90 750,000 1/16 J.B.C. & A. Forms/C.2118/12.

B.E.F.

SUMMARY OF MEDICAL WAR DIARIES OF 2/3rd H.C.F.A. 58th Div.

18th Corps. 5th ARMY.

Western Front Operations - Aug.-Sept. 1917.

Officer Commanding - Lt.Col. J. Barkley.

SUMMARISED UNDER THE FOLLOWING HEADINGS :-

Phase "D" 1. Passchendaele Operations, "July - Nov. 1917."

(a) - Operations commencing July 30th 1917.

B.E.F.

2/3rd H.C.F.A. 58th Div. — Western Front

18th Corps. 5th ARMY. — Aug-Sept. 1917.

O .C. Lt.Col. J. Barkley.

PHASE "D" 1. - Passchendaele Operations,"July-Nov. 1917."

(a) - Operations commencing July 1st 1917.

Headquarters at L'Ebbe Farm Poperinghe.

Aug. 25th. Moves and Transfer. Unit transferred with 58th Div. from 17th Corps III. Army to 18th Corps 5th Army and moved to L'Ebbe Farm.

29th. Moves. To A.D.S. Duhallow C.25.d.3.2.

Medical Arrangements. Adv. Posts east of Yser Canal taken over from 1/2nd S.M.F.A.

Casualties R.A.M.C. 0 & 2 killed. 0 & 1 wounded.

Sept. 2nd.	Casualties R.A.M.C.	Lt.Col. J. Barkley slightly wounded remained at duty.
		Capt. Maile wounded.
	Medical Arrangements.	Bearers 2/1st H.C.F.A. relieved Bearers 2/3rd H.C.F.A. in line.
4th.	Medical Arrangements.	Bearers 2/2nd H.C.F.A. relieved Brs 2/1st H.C.F.A. in line.
6th.	Casualties R.A.M.C.	0 & 2 wounded.
7th.	Casualties R.A.M.C., Gas.	0 & 3 2/2nd H.C.F.A. gassed.
8th.	Casualties R.A.M.C.	0 & 1 wounded.
9th.		0 & 1 wounded.
11th.		0 & 1 wounded.
15th.	Medical Arrangements.	Bearers 2/3rd H.C.F.A. relieved Bearers 2/2nd H.C.F.A. in line.
	Casualties R.A.M.C.	0 & 1 wounded.

2/3rd H.C.F.A. 58th Div. Western Front.

18th Corps. 5th ARMY. Aug.-Sept. 1917.

O.C. Lt.Col. J. BARKLEY.

PHASE "D" 1.- Passchendaele Operations, "July-Nov. 1917."

(a) - Operations commencing July ~~1917~~ 1917.

Headquarters at A.D.S. Duhallow C.25.d.3.2.

Sept. 16th. Casualties R.A.M.C. Capt. Bull attached 2/3rd London Regiment killed.

0 & 2 wounded.

19th. Medical Arrangements. Assistance.) All R.A.M.C. Bearers on routes of evacuation relieved by Stretcher Bearers of 2/9th London Regiment. 3 & 176.

20th. Operations R.A.M.C. Sgt. Smith A.G. captured 2 German Medical Officers. Quantity of Medical Stores captured at Hubner Fm. D.1.b.4.8.

Medical Arrangements. 80 R.A.M.C. Bearers sent to forward area to collect any wounded lying out.

22nd. Medical Arrangements. All R.A.M.C. Bearers and R.S.B's withdrawn from line.

24th. Operations Enemy. Ad. Collecting Post California heavily shelled. 3 Ford Ambulances destroyed - 2 large ambulances damaged. Kitchen and part of dressing room blown up.

Casualties R.A.M.C. 0 & 4 wounded.

B.E.F.

2/3rd H.C.F.A. 58th Div. Western Front.

18th Corps. 5th Army. Aug.-Sept. 1917.
O.C. - Lt.Col. J. Barkley.
To 19th Corps 5th Army from 28th Sept.

PHASE "D" 1. - Passchendaele Operations, "July-Nov. 1917."

(a) - Operations commencing July 1st 1917.

Headquarters at A.D.S. Duhallow C.25.d.3.2.

Sept. 24th. Casualties. A.S.C. attached. 0 & 5 wounded.

Moves Detachment. 1 & 19 to 4th C.C.S.

25th. Medical Arrangements. 72 Bearers sent up to reinforce line.

Operations Enemy. A.D.Col. P. heavily shelled.

Casualties R.A.M.C. 0 & 1 wounded.

Casualties A.S.C. attached. 0 & 1 wounded.

26th. Medical Arrangements. 40 bearers sent to Janet Farm. C.25.d.3.0.

15 Squads Bearers sent to Forward Area during day.

Casualties R.A.M.C. 0 & 1 killed. 0 & 3 wounded.

27th. Medical Arrangements. 4 squads Bearers sent to Forward Area.

Casualties. 9 p.m. 26th to 9 a.m. 27th 101 wounded passed through A.D.C.P.

28th. Medical Arrangements. All forward posts handed over to 1/3rd S.M.F.A.

Moves. To Gwent Farm A.28,a.5.5. (Sheet 28).

~~and Transfer. To 19th Corps V. Army.~~

2/3rd H.C.F.A. 58th Div. Western Front.

18th Corps. 5th ARMY. Aug.-Sept. 1917.

O.C. Lt.Col. J. BARKLEY.

PHASE "D" 1.- Passchendaele Operations,"July-Nov. 1917."

(a) - Operations commencing July 31st 1917.

Headquarters at A.D.S. Duhallow C.25.d.3.2.

Sept. 16th. Casualties R.A.M.C. Capt. Bull attached 2/3rd London Regiment killed.
0 & 2 wounded.

19th. Medical Arrangements. Assistance.) All R.A.M.C. Bearers on routes of evacuation relieved by Stretcher Bearers of 2/9th London Regiment. 3 & 176.

20th. Operations R.A.M.C. Sgt. Smith A.G. captured 2 German Medical Officers. Quantity of Medical Stores captured at Hubner Fm. 1.b.4.8.

Medical Arrangements. 80 R.A.M.C. Bearers sent to forward area to collect any wounded lying out.

22nd. Medical Arrangements. All R.A.M.C. Bearers and R.S.B's withdrawn from line.

24th. Operations Enemy. Ad. Collecting Post California heavily shelled. 3 Ford Ambulances destroyed - 2 large ambulances damaged. Kitchen and part of dressing room blown up.

Casualties R.A.M.C. 0 & 4 wounded.

2/3rd H.C.F.A. 58th Div. Western Front.

18th Corps. 5th Army. Aug.-Sept. 1917.
O.C. - Lt.Col. J. Barkley.
To 19th Corps 5th Army from 28th Sept.

PHASE "D" 1. - Passchendaele Operations, "July-Nov. 1917.

(a) - Operations commencing July/31 1917.

Headquarters at A.D.S. Duhallow C.25.d.2.2.

Sept. 24th. Casualties. A.S.C. attached. 0 & 5 wounded.

Moves Detachment. 1 & 19 to 4th C.C.S.

25th. Medical Arrangements. 72 Bearers sent up to reinforce line.

Operations Enemy. A.D.Col. P. heavily shelled.

Casualties R.A.M.C. 0 & 1 wounded.

Casualties A.S.C. attached. 0 & 1 wounded.

26th. Medical Arrangements. 40 bearers sent to Janet Farm. C.25.d.3.0.

15 Squads Bearers sent to Forward Area during day.

Casualties R.A.M.C. 0 & 1 killed. 0 & 3 wounded.

27th. Medical Arrangements. 4 squads Bearers sent to Forward Area.

Casualties. 9 p.m. 26th to 9 a.m. 27th 101 wounded passed through A.D.C.P.

28th. Medical Arrangements. All forward posts handed over to 1/3rd S.M.F.A.

Moves. To Gwent Farm A.28,a.5.5. (Sheet 28).
~~and Transfer. To 19th Corps V. Army.~~

Gt.197
5

14 0/2 + 97

2/2nd Home Counties F.A.

8

Army Form C. 2118.

Instructions regarding War Diaries and Intelligence Summaries are contained in F. S. Regs., Part II. and the Staff Manual respectively. Title Pages will be prepared in manuscript.

WAR DIARY
or
INTELLIGENCE SUMMARY
(Erase heading not required.)

Vol 9

Place	Date	Hour	Summary of Events and Information	Remarks and references to Appendices
			WAR DIARY - MEDICAL -	
			OF	
			2/3rd HOME COUNTIES FIELD AMBULANCE	
			RAMC T.F.	
			OCTOBER	
			1917	

2449 Wt. W14957/M90 750,000 1/16 J.B.C. & A. Forms/C.2118/12.

Army Form C. 2118.

WAR DIARY

or

~~INTELLIGENCE SUMMARY~~

(Erase heading not required.)

Instructions regarding War Diaries and Intelligence Summaries are contained in F. S. Regs., Part II. and the Staff Manual respectively. Title Pages will be prepared in manuscript.

Place	Date	Hour	Summary of Events and Information	Remarks and references to Appendices
GWENT FARM. SHEET 28 A 28. a 5.5.	1-10.17	10 p.m.	left for PESELHOEK STATION ~~where~~ personnel were to entrain at 11 p.m. All equipment and camp handed over to 1/1st S.M.F.A.	
BLANC PIGNON HAZEBROUCK 5a 2 B O 4.	1.10.17	4.30 p.m.	Transport section arrived.	
	1.10.17	-	Capt. Harris S.M. RAMC T.C. Capt Gilmore T.J. RAMC T.C. Lt Blair G. RAMC T.C. reported for duty.	
do.	2.10.17	noon	Personnel which proceeded by train on 1/10/17 arrived. Billet No 3. taken over as Headquarters. Sick to be accommodated by us for 24 hours before being evacuated to CRS or CCS. Two rooms set aside for this purpose	
do.	3.10.17	11 am.	DDMS XIX Corps & ADMS 58th DIV ~~visited~~ Headquarters. Building to be turned into a reception Hospital. Every patient to be kept for 14 days before transfer to CCS or CRS except in special cases.	
do.	2.10.17		Capt. A. HAYES SMITH evacuated sick.	
do.	2.10.17		Capt Gilmore T.J. RAMC T.C. Lt Blair G. RAMC T.C. proceeded for duty with ADMS. 48th DIV.	
do.	8.10.17		LT. Col. BARKLEY J proceeded on 10 days leave to England. Capt. LEESON. H.W. acting as O/c.	
do.	10.10.17		DDMS. XIX Corps visited Headquarters.	
do.	10.10.17		Capt. GILMORE. T.J. RAMC T.C. LT BLAIR. G. RAMC T.C. returned from duty with 48th DIVN.	
do.	11.10.17		LT BLAIR G RAMC T.C. posted to 2/1 H.C.F.A. for duty.	
do.	12.10.17		CAPT GILMORE T J RAMC T.C. sent to Fifth Army Rest camp for duty.	
do.	13.10.17		Capt. GAWN. R.D. R.A.M.C. T.F. reported for duty. also 12 reinforcements.	
do.	18.10.17		A.D.M.S. + DADMS. 58th DIV. visited Headquarters.	
do	19.10.17		Patients from 2/1st & 2/2nd H.C.F.A. transferred to us. Operation Orders re move to new area received. LT. Col. BARKLEY J. returned from leave.	
do.	20.10.17	8 am	Advanced Party proceeded to new area.	
		8.30 am	Transport proceeded by road to new area.	
do	21.10.17	3 pm	C.O. and motor Ambulance by road to new area.	
	21.10.17	midnight	Main body by ~~train~~ to new area.	

2449 Wt. W14957/M90 750,000 1/16 J.B.C. & A. Forms/C.2118/12.

Army Form C. 2118.

Instructions regarding War Diaries and Intelligence Summaries are contained in F. S. Regs., Part II. and the Staff Manual respectively. Title Pages will be prepared in manuscript.

WAR DIARY
or
~~INTELLIGENCE SUMMARY~~
(Erase heading not required.)

Place	Date	Hour	Summary of Events and Information	Remarks and references to Appendices
ROAD CAMP Sheet 27. L. 1a	22-10-17	11 am	Main body reported. AD	
		noon	A.D.M.S. 58th DIVN visited camp and warned us we were to move to GWENT FARM, Sheet 28. ~~R~~. 26 a. 5.5 in morning. AD	
do	.	7 pm	Order for C.O. 2nd in Command + one officer to be prepared to visit the routes of evacuation at 10 am 23-10-17. AD	
do	23-10-17	10 am	C.O. + 2nd in Command proceeded to visit the routes of evacuation. AD	
do		11 am	Main body + transport proceed to GWENT FARM. AD	
GWENT FARM Sheet 28 [illegible]		noon.	Main body + transport arrived. Tent sub division rejoined from 44 CCS. AD	
do.	24-10-17	11 am	A.D.M.S 58th DIV visited Headquarters. AD	
		4 pm	Bearers of 2/2 H.C.F.A. despatched to ISLAY FARM. AD	
		5 pm	Capt. LEESON to forward area. AD	
		6 pm	C.C. to forward area AD	
Sheet 28. C.19 C.3.0. ESSEX FARM	25-10-17	10 am.	Headquarters of Unit transferred to C.19 C.3.0. AD	
			Bearers of 2/2 H.C.F.A. took over + manned the routes of evacuation. AD	
		11.30 am	C.O. visited forward area and routes of evacuation	
do		2.30 pm	C.O. to GWENT FARM re having more bearers sent forward.	
do		3 pm	12 squads sent up to reinforce line (2/2 H.C.F.A men) AD	
do	26-10-17	5 am	12 squads sent up to reinforce line (2/2 H.C.F.A men)	
		7 am	8 men (2/2 H.C.F.A) evacuated N.Y.D. Gas poisoning. 3 men (2/2 H.C.F.A) evacuated wounded.	
		11 am	C.O. and A.D.M.S 58th Divn to forward area.	
		6 pm	1 man (2/2 H.C.F.A) evacuated N.Y.D. Gas poisoning. also 2 men 2/2 H.C.F.A. AD	
do	27-10-17	4 am	C.O. + A.D.M.S. 58th Divn visited posts + routes of evacuation.	
		10 am	Capt. White, posted for duty with 2/4 London Regt.	
		10 am	6 men (2/2 H.C.F.A) evacuated with N.Y.D. Gas poisoning. AD	

2449 Wt. W14957/M90 750,000 1/16 J.B.C. & A. Forms/C.2118/12.

Instructions regarding War Diaries and Intelligence Summaries are contained in F. S. Regs., Part II. and the Staff Manual respectively. Title Pages will be prepared in manuscript.

WAR DIARY
or
~~INTELLIGENCE~~ SUMMARY

(Erase heading not required.)

Army Form C. 2118.

Place	Date	Hour	Summary of Events and Information	Remarks and references to Appendices
ESSEX FARM. SHEET. 28. C.19.c 3.0	27.10.17		Lt ORTON. W.H. RAM.C T.C. sent back to rest with N.Y.D. Gas Poisoning also 1 N.C.O.	
		7 pm	2 men evacuated wounded. Great difficulty, owing to mud, in evacuating the wounded. mud sleighs sent forward.	
do	28-10-17	10 am	A.D.M.S. 58th Divn and C.O. to forward area.	
		5 pm	1 S.Sgt killed + 7 other ranks wounded at U.30.d.6.9.	
do	29-10-17	12.35 am	Capt. ELLIOTT RAMC T.C. proceeded to England.	
		4 am	C.O. + A.D.M.S. 58th Divn to forward area.	
		noon	3 men (2/3 H.C.F.A) killed in action. 3 other ranks wounded.	
		6.30 pm	R.A.M.C. bearers in the line relieved by Regimental stretcher bearers of 173rd I. Bde. 15 squads (2/3 H.C.F.A) proceeded into the line.	
do	30-10-17	9 am	A.D.M.S. 58th Divn + C.O. to forward area.	
		noon	10 squads R.A.M.C. bearers reported at ISLAY FARM.	
		"	35 squads R.S.B.'s reported at ISLAY FARM.	
do.	31-10-17	5 am	C.O. + A.D.M.S. 58th Divn proceeded to forward area.	
		8 am	8 men reported suffering from N.Y.D. Gas poisoning. 1 evacuated, remainder sent to GWENT FARM for rest. 1 other rank wounded + evacuated. 1 O.R. Killed	
		3 pm	R.A.M.C. bearers relieved in the line. 40 R.S.B.'s relieved + sent back to Unit.	

[illegible]
Lieut Col
OC 2/3 HCF Amb

5

140/2578.

2/3rd Home Counties F.A.

7

Instructions regarding War Diaries and Intelligence Summaries are contained in F. S. Regs., Part II. and the Staff Manual respectively. Title Pages will be prepared in manuscript.

WAR DIARY
or
INTELLIGENCE SUMMARY

(Erase heading not required.)

2/3RD HOME COUNTIES FIELD AMBULANCE.
No.
Date

Army Form C. 2118.

Vol 10

Place	Date	Hour	Summary of Events and Information	Remarks and references to Appendices

CONFIDENTIAL.

WAR DIARY

OF

2/3RD HOME COUNTIES FIELD AMBULANCE.

FROM NOVEMBER 1ST 1917 TO NOVEMBER 30TH 1917

MEDICAL.

J Heckley
LIEUT. COL.
O.C. 2ND/3RD HOME COUNTIES
FIELD AMBULANCE R.A.M.C.

2449 Wt. W14957/M90 750,000 1/16 J.B.C. & A. Forms/C.2118/12.

Army Form C. 2118.

WAR DIARY
or
INTELLIGENCE SUMMARY
(Erase heading not required.)

Instructions regarding War Diaries and Intelligence Summaries are contained in F. S. Regs., Part II. and the Staff Manual respectively. Title Pages will be prepared in manuscript.

2/3RD HOME COUNTIES FIELD AMBULANCE.
No.
Date

Place	Date	Hour	Summary of Events and Information	Remarks and references to Appendices
Sheet 28. C.19.c.3.0 ESSEX FARM.	1-11-17		A.D.M.S. + C.O. visited forward area + lines of evacuation. 1st Lt. FROST M.O.R.C. U.S.A. relieved Capt GAWN R.D. in the line. [initials]	
do	2-11-17	5 am	R.A.M.C. bearers relieved Regimental stretcher bearers on the routes of evacuation. R.S.B's to GWENT forward. Capt. ROGERS F.E.W. relieved Capt. LEESON H. as Officer i/c bearers who proceeded to GWENT. [initials]	
		noon	Capt. GAWN R.D. to GWENT for rest. [initials]	
do	3-11-17	noon	D.D.M.S. II Corps at ESSEX FARM.	
do	4-11-17	5 am	bearers relieved in the line. [initials]	
		2 pm	200 men + 2 officers of 7/5th LONDON REGT reported at A.28.a.5.5 to relieve men of 173rd I. Bde acting as bearers.	
		5 pm	Capt. ROGERS F.E.W. reported that R.A.P's at V.19.a.7.1. and GLOSTER FARM. V.20.c.4.2 were being evacuated and that PHEASANT TRENCH U.30.d.6.9 was to be used as R.A.P. A.D.M.S. 58 Div ordered that GLOSTER FARM shall be kept on as a RELAY POSTS. RELAY POSTS at U.29.b.8.2. and C.4.b.5.5. evacuated. Surplus bearers sent to BULOW FARM. C.6.a.8.8. in reserve. [initials]	
do	5-11-17	8 am	Capt. LEESON relieved Capt. ROGERS F. as O i/c of Bearers.	
		10 am	A.D.M.S. 58th Div and C.O. to the forward area. [initials]	
do	6-11-17	5 am	2 Regimental Officers and 200 men acting as bearers relieved bearers in the line. [initials]	
do	8-11-17	5 am	50 R.A.M.C. bearers relieved regimental stretcher bearers in the line.	
		noon	Men acting as bearers of 7/5 London Regt withdrawn.	
		2.30 pm	100 men of 7/4 London Regt reported for duty as stretcher bearers. [initials]	
do	10-11-17	5 am	80 Regimental bearers relieved R.A.M.C. bearers in the line. 1st Lt DOOLING J.F. M.O.R.C. U.S.A. joined Unit.	
		10 am	C.O. to forward area. 2 men 7/4 London Regt wounded. One man 2/1st H.C.F.A. killed. [initials]	
do	11-11-17	9 am	Capt Rogers F.E.W. relieved Capt Leeson as Officer i/c bearers. [initials]	
do	12-11-17	7 am	50 R.A.M.C. bearers relieved R.S.B's of 7/4 London Regt. who proceeded to GWENT. [initials]	
do	13-11-17	9 am	C.O. to forward area. Capt. GAMM F. R.A.M.C. S.R. joined Unit for duty.	
		9 pm	Handed over route of evacuation to O/c 2/2nd H.C.F.A. [initials]	
do.	14-11-17	9 am	C.O. + Headquarters moved to GWENT FARM. [initials]	

2149 Wt. W14957/M90 750,000 1/16 J.B.C. & A. Forms/C.2118/12.

Instructions regarding War Diaries and Intelligence Summaries are contained in F. S. Regs., Part II. and the Staff Manual respectively. Title Pages will be prepared in manuscript.

WAR DIARY
or
INTELLIGENCE SUMMARY
(Erase heading not required.)

2/3RD HOME COUNTIES FIELD AMBULANCE.
No.
Date

Army Form C. 2118.

Place	Date	Hour	Summary of Events and Information	Remarks and references to Appendices
Sheet 28. a. 28. a. 0. 5	14-11-17	10.30am	Unit moved to Proven Area. (less 80 bearers handed over to 1/2nd H.C. F.A. for duty on routes of evacuation). JH	
Sheet 27. F. 1. b. 3. 2. PORTEEA CAMP	14.11.17	2 pm	Unit arrived from GWENT FARM. JH	
do.	17-11-17	noon	Capt. ROGERS. F.E.W. + bearers rejoined Unit from duty in forward area. JH	
do.	20-11-17	10am	C.O. inspected Medical Equipment of 2/9th, 2/10th & 2/11th London Regts. + noted deficiencies. JH	
do	20-11-17	6 pm	Movement Order No. 56. of 175th I Bde re move of advance parties to new area received. JH	
do.	21-11-17		Lt F POOLE to England on leave - 14 days. JH	
do	20-11-17	7am	Advance Party of 1 Officer; 4 other ranks proceeded to new area. JH	
do	24-11-17	11am	C.O. with advanced party to new area. Area to which advanced party proceeded on 22-11-17 cancelled. JH	
do	26-11-17	8 am	All transport by road to LUMBRES Area along with 175th I. Bde Transport. JH	
do.	27-11-17	1 pm	Personnel entrained at PROVEN Station for LUMBRES AREA. JH	
LART HAZEBROUCK 5A 4. a. b. 3	28-11-17	12 30am	Personnel arrived at LART. JH	
	29-11-17	2.30pm	A.D.M.S. 58th DIV visited Field Ambulance Area. JH	
		11 pm	Orders received for Field Ambulance to move to CHATEAU, AFFRINGUES. JH	
do	30-11-17	8.30am	Field Ambulance moved to CHATEAU, AFFRINGUES. Chateau to be opened as D.R.S. to accomodate 80 patients. JH	
AFFRINGUES HAZEBROUCK 5A 4. b. 1. 4.	"	11.35am	Move completed. All billets at LART evacuated. Personnel billeted at Chateau and St PIERRE. JH	

JHartley
LIEUT. COL.
O.C. 2nd/3rd HOME COUNTIES FIELD AMBULANCE R.A.M.C.

2449 Wt. W14957/M90 750,000 1/16 J.B.C. & A. Forms/C.2118/12.

Doc. 91

5

140/2018

2/3rd Home Counties F. A.

Army Form C. 2118.

WAR DIARY
or
INTELLIGENCE SUMMARY

(Erase heading not required.)

Ins[illegible]ions regarding War Diaries and Intelligence Summaries are contained in F. S. Regs., Part II. and the Staff Manual respectively. Title Pages will be prepared in manuscript.

2/3RD HOME COUNTIES FIELD AMBULANCE.
No.......
Date.......

Vol 11

Place	Date	Hour	Summary of Events and Information	Remarks and references to Appendices
HAZEBROUCK 5A 4.B.4.4 AFFRINGUES.	1.12.17	2 pm	Headquarters of Unit transferred to ST PIERRE. HAZEBROUCK 5A 4.a.9.2 Chateau LANNOY. AFFRINGUES to be used as Divl Rest Station.	
do	4.12.17		Operation Orders of 175th I Bde received re move of Unit with Brigade to new area.	
do	4.12.17		Lt Cavanagh, MORC, USA transferred to New Zealand Stationary Hospital WISQUES sick.	
do	5.12.17	9 am	Horse transport less 1 GS wagon, 2 limbers and 3 water carts left Headquarters to join 175th I Bde convoy en route to new area.	
			Lt WARD & Lt LEES, MORC USA with 62 other ranks joined Unit for temporary duty.	
		2 pm	Orders received for the Divl Rest Station to be evacuated and all patients transferred to New Zealand Stationary Hospital, WISQUES.	
do	6.12.17	5 pm	Lt CAVE RP & Lt DOOLING F MORC USA transferred for temporary duty with II Corps Rest Camp HERZEELE.	
		4.10 am	1 GS limbered wagon, 2 water carts with personnel left Unit en route for new area by Omnibus train.	
		9 am	Personnel of Unit move off to LUMBRES Cross Roads where they were embussed & taken to WIZERNE STATION en route for new area. Motor Ambulances by road.	
		11 am	1 GS wagon, 1 limbered GS wagon, 1 water cart with personnel joining column of 2/2nd HCFA at ~~[illegible]~~ BAYENHEM en route for new area.	
GWENT FARM. Sheet 28 R.29.a.5.5	6.12.17	5 pm	Personnel of Unit arrived. 6 pm transport which travelled by omnibus train reported.	
do	7.12.17	9 am	CO proceeded to the forward zone.	
do	8.12.17	9 am	Bearers of 2/3 HCFA with two tent sub divisions & 12 bearers of 2/2nd HCFA proceeded to take over forward Area. Capt Gaunn F RAMC SR in charge of Left sector with Advanced Dressing Station at CEMENT HOUSE U.28.c.2.2 Sheet 20; Lieut Ward RAMC in charge of Centre sector with ADS at MINTY FARM C.10.c.3.0 Sheet 28, and Capt Leeson RAMC in charge of right sector with ADS at ST JULIEN C.18.a.1.7 Sheet 28.	
do		noon	Headquarters of Unit transferred to Essex Farm. Sheet 28 C.19.c 3.0.	
ESSEX FARM Sheet 28 C.19.c 3.0	8.12.17		CO to forward areas and along the routes of evacuation.	
do	9.12.17	9 am	CO to forward area.	

Instructions regarding War Diaries and Intelligence Summaries are contained in F. S. Regs., Part II. and the Staff Manual respectively. Title Pages will be prepared in manuscript.

WAR DIARY
or
INTELLIGENCE SUMMARY
(Erase heading not required.)

2/3RD HOME COUNTIES FIELD AMBULANCE. No. .... Date ....

Army Form C. 2118.

Place	Date	Hour	Summary of Events and Information	Remarks and references to Appendices
ESSEX FARM. Sht 28. C.19.c.3.0	9-12-17	10 am	Relief of all personnel in forward area and at A.D.S.'s complete.	
do	10-12-17	9 am	A.D.M.S. 58th Divn & C.O. to forward area. LTs CAVE & DOOLING returned from II Corps Rest Camp.	
do	11-12-17	6 am	Personnel at A.D.S. St JULIEN and at forward posts on this sector relieved by a Field Ambulance of 32nd Divn.	
do	11-12-17	6 am	All routes of evacuation handed over to 2/1st H.C.F.A R.A.M.C.	
GWENT FARM. Sheet 28. A.22.a.5.5	11-12-17	9 am	Unit move to CANADA FARM Sheet 28 A.18.a.2.7. and took over Divisional Rest Station from 106th Field Ambulance.	
CANADA FARM Sheet 28. A.18.a.2.7.	"	noon	Move completed.	
do.	12-12-17	9 am	Men of bearer divisions of Field Ambulance handed over to 2/1st H.C.F.A. for duty in forward area.	
do.	"	noon	Daily State. Rming O.R. 125. Admd. 1 officer. 56 O.R. To C.C.S. 1 officer 6 O.R. Rming. 175 O.R.	
"	13-12-17	2.20 pm	A.D.M.S. 58th Divn visited Rest Station	
do	"	noon	Daily State. Rmnd. 175 OR; admd 2 officers. 43 OR; To C.C.S 1 officer 6 OR; To CRS. 16 OR. To duty 32. Rming 1 off. 164 OR.	
do.	14-12-17	9 am	1st LT CAVE RR; M.O.R.C.; U.S.A. detailed for duty with 58th Divl. R. E.	
do.	14-12-17	noon	Daily State. Rmnd 1 officer. 164 OR; Admd 3 officers 33 OR To C.C.S. 2 officers 4 OR. To CRS. 12 OR. To duty 11 OR. Rming 2 off. 170 OR.	
do.	14-12-17	2 pm	A.D.M.S. & D.A.D.M.S. 58th Divn visited Rest station	
do	15-12-17	noon	Daily State. Rmnd 2 off. 170 OR Admd 31 OR. To C.C.S. 7 OR To CRS 2 OR To duty 15 OR. Rming 2 officers 194 OR.	
do	16-12-17	"	Daily State. Rmnd. 2 off. 194 OR Admd. 1 off. 49 OR. To C.C.S 11 OR. To CR.S 1 off. 5 OR To duty 10 OR Rming. 2 off. 208 OR.	
do	17-12-17	"	Daily State. Rmnd. 2 off. 208 OR. Admd 1 off. 39 OR. To C.C.S 16 OR To CRS 9 OR To duty 2 OR. Rming. 3 off. 220 OR.	
do	18-12-17	"	Daily State. Rmnd. 3 off. 220 OR. Admd. 1 off. 51 OR. To C.C.S 1 off. 22 OR. To CRS. 8 OR To duty 14 OR. Rming 3 off. 227 OR.	
do.	19-12-17	"	Daily State. Rmnd. 3 off. 227 OR. Admd 1 off. 42 OR. To C.C.S. 5 OR. To CRS. 1 off. 24 OR. To duty 14 OR. Rming 3 off. 226 OR.	
do	"	2 pm	A.D.M.S. 58th Divn visited Rest Station	

2449 Wt. W14957/M90 750,000 1/16 J.B.C. & A. Forms/C.2118/12.

Instructions regarding War Diaries and Intelligence Summaries are contained in F. S. Regs., Part II. and the Staff Manual respectively. Title Pages will be prepared in manuscript.

WAR DIARY
or
INTELLIGENCE SUMMARY

(Erase heading not required.)

2/3RD HOME COUNTIES FIELD AMBULANCE.
No.........
Date.........

Army Form C. 2118.

Place	Date	Hour	Summary of Events and Information	Remarks and references to Appendices
CANADA FARM. Sheet 28. A.18.a.2.7	20.12.17	noon	Daily State. Remg. 3 off 236 OR. Admd 43 OR. To CCS 11 OR. To CRS 3 off 49 OR. To duty 10 OR. Remg 199 OR.	[initials]
do	21.12.17	noon	Daily State Remd 199 OR. Admd 1 off 39 OR. To CCS 6 OR. To CRS 1 off 4 OR. To duty 9 OR. Remg 209 OR. ADMS 58th Divn visited DRS. DDMS II Corps visited DRS.	[initials]
"	22.12.17	noon	Numbers of Trench Foot cases increasing. ADMS 58th Divn visited Trench Foot ward. Erection of stage in dining & recreation room completed. Stores buildings & [illegible] boards removed from SOLFERINO FM.	[initials]
	23.12.17	noon	No Church Parade owing to Dining Hall floor being cemented. [illegible] 58th Divn visited DRS. Patients in Hospital 271 patients. 2 off + 45 OR admitted. Evacuations 2 off 35 OR. Duty 7 OR. [initials]	
"	24.12.17	"	Evacuations 66 OR. Duty 11. Patients & Personnel engaged in preparing DRS for Christmas. The NISSEN HUT erected at pack store. 255 Patients in Hosp. Admissions 61. Band of 2/10 Lond Watt. lent to 7 Amb for 8 days.	[initials]
	25.12.17	"	ADMS ADC & QMG 58th Divn visited DRS after Xmas dinner. Church Parade. GOC. Patients in Hospital GOC expressed appreciation of the place & remarked on cleanliness. Concert for patients given by Remg 289. Adm 1 off 58 OR. Evac. 1 off 24 OR. Duty nil. & one patient. Band. Band. [initials]	
	26.12.17	"	294 Patients in Hosp. Adm. 3 off 63 OR. Evac. 2 off 36 OR. Duty 22. Snow on ground & very cold. Great scarcity of lighting oil & coal. Coal question remedied by station that DRS is a Hospital so that a special allowance may be drawn. 7 tons per week. [initials]	
	27.12.17	"	296 Patients in Hosp. 69 OR admitted. Evacuated 39 OR. Duty 28. DDMS II Corps visited Hosp & directed that patients were not to be kept except under special circumstances over five days. They were then to be transferred to II Corps rest Station.	[initials]
	28.12.17	"	296 Patients in Hosp. Adm. 4 off 52 OR. Evac. 3 off 49 OR. Duty 42. Visited by direction of DDMS, II Corps rest station. Dentist at DRS in am. [initials]	
	29.12.17	"	Remaining 257 [initials]	
	30.12.17	"	Church Parade C of E & Presbyterian at 10 am & 11 am. [initials]	
	31.12.17	"	DDMS 58th Divn visited DRS & inspected wards 3 & 4. Dentist from II Corps attended DRS this morning. 15 cases sent to MONT DES CATS for [illegible] treatment.	

J. H. Barkley Lt. Col.
OC 2/3 HC F Amb

2149 Wt. W14957/M90 750,000 1/16 J.B.C. & A. Forms/C.2118/12.

9

Instructions regarding War Diaries and Intelligence Summaries are contained in F. S. Regs., Part II. and the Staff Manual respectively. Title Pages will be prepared in manuscript.

WAR DIARY
or
INTELLIGENCE SUMMARY

(Erase heading not required.)

2/3RD HOME COUNTIES FIELD AMBULANCE.

Army Form C. 2118.

Vol 12

Place	Date	Hour	Summary of Events and Information	Remarks and references to Appendices
Jan. 1918			140/2696	

CONFIDENTIAL

WAR DIARY

of

2/3RD HOME COUNTIES FIELD AMBULANCE

R.A.M.C. T.

FROM JANUARY 1ST 1918 to JANUARY 31ST 1918.

[signature]
LIEUT. COL.
O.C. 2ND/3RD HOME COUNTIES FIELD AMBULANCE R.A.M.C.

2449 Wt. W14957/M90 750,000 1/16 J.B.C. & A. Forms/C.2118/12.

Instructions regarding War Diaries and Intelligence Summaries are contained in F. S. Regs., Part II. and the Staff Manual respectively. Title Pages will be prepared in manuscript.

WAR DIARY
or
~~INTELLIGENCE SUMMARY~~
(Erase heading not required.)

2/3RD HOME COUNTIES FIELD AMBULANCE.

No. ....
Date ....

Army Form C. 2118.

Place	Date	Hour	Summary of Events and Information	Remarks and references to Appendices
58th D.R.S. CANADA Fm. Sh 28 A 18 a 27.	1.1.18	noon	233 in Hospital. Yesterday afternoon ADMS visited Divisional Rest Station on his return from leave. Building [illegible] [illegible]. Frost very severe this morning. Arranged supply of fresh milk with farm at 5d per litre.	
do.	2.1.18	"	223 in Hosp. 47 OR adm. 27 transferred. 23 to duty.	
do	5.1.18	.	Capt. Lesson A.H. posted for duty with VIII Corps.	
do	6.1.18	11 am	Phone message received to send an Advanced Party to take over Rest Station at HERZEELE.	
		2 pm.	Advanced Party proceeded.	
do	7.1.18	10 am	Transport proceeded by road to new area.	
		1 pm	Personnel of Unit proceeded to new Area.	
		noon.	Divl. Rest Station at CANADA FARM handed over to 105th F.A.	
58th D.R.S. Sht 27. C.10.c.1.6	8.1.18	noon	Patients in Hospital 13.	
do	9.1.18	noon	Patients in Hospital 19.	
do	10.1.18	noon	A.D.M.S. 58th Divn visited Rest Station.	
do	11.1.18	2 pm.	Officers attended a lecture of 58th Divl. medical Socy. at 12 C.C.S. Subject. - Trench feet.	
do	12.1.18	noon	Daily State. Remd. 29. Admd. 7. C.C.S. 1. Remg. 45.	
do	13.1.18	noon	Daily State. Remd. 45. Admd. 5. C.C.S. 5. Remg. 45.	
do	14.1.18	noon	Daily State. Remd. 45. Admd. 7. C.C.S. 2. C.S.Dot. 1. Duty 2. Remg. 47.	
do	14.1.18		Orders received re move to new Area. Probably date 20.1.18.	
do	15.1.18	noon	Daily State. Remd. 47. Admd. 12. C.C.S. 8. duty 2. Remg. 49.	
		2 pm	Officers attended lecture of 58th Divl. Medical Socy at 12 C.C.S. - subject P.U.O.	
		5 pm	Order received for Adv. Party for new Area to proceed at 5.30 pm.	
		5.30 pm	Lt. Poole + 6 OR proceeded by rail to new Area as Advanced Party.	

2149 Wt. W14957/M90 750,000 1/16 J.B.C. & A. Forms/C.2118/12.

Instructions regarding War Diaries and Intelligence Summaries are contained in F. S. Regs., Part II. and the Staff Manual respectively. Title Pages will be prepared in manuscript.

WAR DIARY
or
~~INTELLIGENCE SUMMARY~~
(Erase heading not required.)

2/3RD HOME COUNTIES FIELD AMBULANCE.
No.
Date

Army Form C. 2118.

Place	Date	Hour	Summary of Events and Information	Remarks and references to Appendices
58th D.R.S. Sht. 27. C.10.c.1.9	15-1-18	9 pm	Administrative instructions for move of 58th Divn to Fifth Army received.	
do.	16-1-18		Great havoc done to Rest Station by storm during the night – marquees blown down and one or two very badly damaged.	
do	17-1-18	noon	A.D.M.S. 58th Divn here – gave orders for all stretchers & blankets & medical comforts to be sent to II C.R.S.; all B.R.C. Stores to be returned and Clayton disinfector to be sent to II Corps Shirt [?] Depot as present site for Rest Station was going to be closed.	
do	18-1-18	noon	Orders for move to Fifth Army Area received.	
do	19-1-18	12.45	Personnel and transport moved off to Central Camps, Proven.	
		5.30 pm	Move completed.	
Central Camps Proven	20-1-18	3.30 am	Transport & loading party arrived at Proven Station for entrainment.	
do		6.30 am	Troops entrained	
		2.30 pm	Mechanical Transport arrived at new destination.	
[illegible] Brettoneux		7.30 pm	Personnel & transport detrained at VILLERS BRETTONEUX Station	
[illegible] 62 D 02. [illegible]	21-1-18	2 am	Move completed.	
		noon	Preparing a place for reception of sick of 175th I. Bde.	
do	22-1-18		1st Lt. Dooling. M.O.R.C., U.S.A. posted for duty with 58th Divl. R.S.	
			1st Lt. [illegible] M.O.R.C., U.S.A. reported for duty.	
			Hospital opened for reception of sick of 175th I Bde.	
do.	23-1-18	11 am	Troops paraded for inspection by G.O.C. 58th Divn. G.O.C. did not arrive.	
do.	25-1-18	9 am	Hospital transferred to CORBIE. C.O. acting A.D.M.S. 58th Divn.	
do.	28-1-18		60 men of the Field Ambulance examined & reclassified.	
do.	31-1-18		Capt. J. G. GILMORE. R.A.M.C. T.F. reported for duty.	
			Lt. CAVANAGH M.O.R.C. U.S.A. reported for duty.	

2449 Wt. W14957/M90 750,000 1/16 J.B.C. & A. Forms/C.2118/12.

14

Instructions regarding War Diaries and Intelligence Summaries are contained in F. S. Regs., Part II. and the Staff Manual respectively. Title Pages will be prepared in manuscript.

WAR DIARY
or
INTELLIGENCE SUMMARY
(Erase heading not required.)

Army Form C. 2118.

Vol 13

Place	Date	Hour	Summary of Events and Information	Remarks and references to Appendices
	Feb. 1918		140/27 84	
			CONFIDENTIAL.	
			WAR DIARY	
			OF	
			2/3rd HOME COUNTIES FIELD AMBULANCE. R.A.M.C. T.F.	
			FROM FEBRUARY 1st 1918 to FEBRUARY 28th 1918.	

John Stuart [signature]
LIEUT. COL.
O.C. 2ND/3RD HOME COUNTIES
FIELD AMBULANCE R.A.M.C.

2449 Wt. W14957/M90 750,000 1/16 J.B.C. & A. Forms/C.2118/12.

Instructions regarding War Diaries and Intelligence Summaries are contained in F. S. Regs., Part II. and the Staff Manual respectively. Title Pages will be prepared in manuscript.

WAR DIARY
or
INTELLIGENCE SUMMARY
(Erase heading not required.)

Army Form C. 2118.

Place	Date	Hour	Summary of Events and Information	Remarks and references to Appendices
Sheet 62D O.2.b.0.7	1.2.18	11 am	G.O.C., 58th DIVN inspected the Field Ambulance on parade in full marching order. Expressed his satisfaction on the turn out.	
do.	2.2.18		Orders received for transport to move to new area in three stages leaving on the 3rd. Advance Party to proceed by lorry on the 4th and main body by train on 6th.	
do.	3.2.18	8 am	Transport, with ~~Capt Gamm~~ Lt Cavanagh i/c, moved off en route for new Area.	
do.	4.2.18	7.15 am	Capt Gamm and 6 OR. as advanced Party left for new area.	
			C.O. proceeded to new area by Car to inspect the ADS's and routes of evacuation to be taken over by this Field Ambulance.	
do.	6.2.17	5.45 am	2 limbers & GS wagon left for CORBIE STATION to entrain to new area	
do.		10 am	Main body proceeded to CORBIE Station to entrain for new area.	
		6 pm.	Troops & transport detrained at APPILLY, and proceeded by march route to VILLEQUIER AUMONT	
		1 am	move complete.	
Sheet 66C S.19.b.5.2 VILLEQUIER AUMONT	6.2.17		Lt. J F DOOLING MORC, USA. rejoined Unit for duty.	
do	7.2.17		Capt. J S WARD RAMC T. reported for duty.	
do	7.2.17	10 am	C.O. Capt Gamm I. & Lt. Dooling to forward area inspecting routes of evacuation and A.D.S's which were being taken over at 2 pm.	
		2 pm	Capt Gamm & personnel for line & ADS proceeded to take over left sector with A.D.S. at REMIGNY Sheet 66C N.14.c.2.6.	
			Capt Ward RAMC T & Lt DOOLING MORC. with personnel for line & ADS proceeded to take over line with A.D.S. at FARGNIERS. Sheet 66C T.27.b.9.9.	
do	8.2.17	9 am	Relief of line complete. Hospital & Headquarters at Sheet 66C S.19.b.5.2 taken over from 2/6th Field Ambulance.	
		10 am	CO to forward Areas with ADMS 58th Division	

Instructions regarding War Diaries and Intelligence Summaries are contained in F. S. Regs., Part II. and the Staff Manual respectively. Title Pages will be prepared in manuscript.

WAR DIARY
or
INTELLIGENCE SUMMARY
(Erase heading not required.)

Army Form C. 2118.

2/3RD HOME COUNTIES FIELD AMBULANCE.
No. ....
Date. ....

Place	Date	Hour	Summary of Events and Information	Remarks and references to Appendices
Sht 66E S.19 b.5.2 VILLEQUIER AUMONT	9.2.18	10 am	CO to forward Area. Orders received to equip line & ADS's with stretchers, each Relay Post with 2 Thomas's splints & each ADS with 6 Thomas's splints.	
		9 pm.	1st Lieut. W B McBEAN & 1st Lieut. Ross M. WILSON, both MORC, USA reported for duty.	
do	10.2.18	9 am	CO with ADMS & DADMS 58th Division to forward area.	
do	11.2.18		CO and Capt. J Ward inspecting routes on evacuation & ADS's	
		2.15 pm	CO and Capt. J. Ward attend conference at CHAUNY.	
do	12.2.18	9 am	Lt Col BARKLEY J. to England on 14 days leave. Capt. J. Ward in temporary command of Unit.	J.S.W.
		noon	ADS, FARGNIERS experiencing great difficulty in evacuating gas cases. Large Cars sent to relieve the congestion.	
		8 pm.	43 cases of gas poisoning dealt with during preceding 24 hours at ADS FARGNIERS	JSW
do	13.2.18	9 am	Capt. J. Ward and DADMS 58th Division to forward area.	
		10 am	Lieut & QM Poole F. evacuated to 46. CCS NOYON.	JSW
do	15.2.18	10 am	CO to Advanced Dressing Stations.	
do.	16.2.18	9 am	1st Lt. LEAS MORC USA proceed on leave to England.	
		11 am	DDMS III Corps & ADMS 58th Div visited headquarters. Spoke about the working of the CRO.	
do.	17.2.18	10 am	CO. to forward area.	
		2.30 pm	CO attending conference at CHAUNY. Lt. WILSON MORC USA + 3 OR attending RAMC course of instruction at HAM.	
do.	18.2.18	10 am	CO. to forward area.	
do	20.2.18	noon	ADS REMIGNY handed over to 43rd Field Ambulance. All personnel with exception of 2 OR withdrawn from ADS. Personnel at Posts in this sector remains the same.	
do	20.2.18	noon	Corps Central Records Office with HQ's at this Field Ambulance opened here.	JSW.

2449 Wt. W14957/M90 750,000 1/16 J.B.C. & A. Forms/C.2118/12.

Instructions regarding War Diaries and Intelligence Summaries are contained in F. S. Regs., Part II. and the Staff Manual respectively. Title Pages will be prepared in manuscript.

WAR DIARY
or
INTELLIGENCE SUMMARY
(Erase heading not required.)

2/3RD HOME COUNTIES FIELD AMBULANCE.
No. ....
Date ....

Army Form C. 2118.

Place	Date	Hour	Summary of Events and Information	Remarks and references to Appendices
Sht 66e S 19. b 5 2 VILLEQUIER AUMONT	21.2.18		Commenced work at making new Collecting Post at Railway Cutting at MENNESSIS Sht 66e M.36.a.7 2. under charge of Capt. GAMM F. Provision being made for 20 stretcher cases, 30 walking wounded, room for 12 Personnel, 2 officers and a dressing Station. J.S.W.	
do.	23.2.18	4 pm	DDMS III Corps visited HQ's.	
		6.30pm	Operation Order No. 37 received re relief of line by 56th Field Ambulance & 2/2 H.C. F.A. by 6pm Field Ambulance on relief to move to MAREST DAMPCOURT.	25/2/17
do.	24.2.18		CO proceeded to MAREST DAMPCOURT to inspect new site of Field Ambulance. JSW	
do	25.2.18	9 am	Hospital and Quarters handed over to 96th Field Ambulance.	
		9.30am	Personnel move off to new area by route march.	
		11 am	Transport moved off.	
MAREST DAMPCOURT Sht 66e L 7. B. 3 a	———	6 pm.	Moved completed also relief of forward area. J.S.W.	
do	27.2.18	~~2pm~~	Lt WILSON M.O.R.C. rejoined from RAMC. course of instruction	
do	28.2.18	2 pm.	Wire received from ADMS, 58th Divn to take precautionary action for Defensive scheme. Reports when Unit is ready to move.	
		3pm	Reported Unit standing by ready to move.	
		5pm	Lt. Col BARKLEY J rejoined from leave. Attending Conference at ADMS 58th Division Office.	

Capt J.S. Ward.
John S Ward Capt RAMC
~~LIEUT. COL.~~
O.C. 2ND/3RD HOME COUNTIES FIELD AMBULANCE R.A.M.C.

1/3/18.

LIEUT. COL.
O.C. 2ND/3RD HOME COUNTIES FIELD AMBULANCE R.A.M.C.

2449 Wt. W14957/M90 750,000 1/16 J.B.C. & A. Forms/C.2118/12.

11

Instructions regarding War Diaries and Intelligence Summaries are contained in F. S. Regs., Part II. and the Staff Manual respectively. Title Pages will be prepared in manuscript.

WAR DIARY
or
INTELLIGENCE SUMMARY

(Erase heading not required.)

Army Form C.

140/2849

Vol 14

Place	Date	Hour	Summary of Events and Information	Remarks and references to Appendices
			CONFIDENTIAL.	
			WAR DIARY	
			of	
			2/3rd HOME COUNTIES FIELD AMBULANCE.	
			R.A.M.C. T.	
			FROM 1st MARCH 1918 to 31st MARCH 1918.	

2/3rd HOME COUNTIES FIELD AMBULANCE.
No. ....
Date ....

J Barkley
LIEUT. COL.
O.C. 2nd/3rd HOME COUNTIES FIELD AMBULANCE R.A.M.C.

2449 Wt. W14957/M90 750,000 1/16 J.B.C. & A. Forms/C.2118/12.

Instructions regarding War Diaries and Intelligence Summaries are contained in F. S. Regs., Part II. and the Staff Manual respectively. Title Pages will be prepared in manuscript.

WAR DIARY
or
~~INTELLIGENCE SUMMARY~~
(Erase heading not required.)

Army Form C. 2118.

2/3RD HOME COUNTIES FIELD AMBULANCE.

Place	Date	Hour	Summary of Events and Information	Remarks and references to Appendices
NEAREST DAMPCOURT Sht. 70c L 7.b.3.0	1-3-18	10am	Capt. Jermin F. took over charge of the ADS FARGNIERS.	
		8pm	Wire from ADMS. 58 Divn received. Act Battle Positions.	
		11pm	Reported Unit ready to move. Personnel dismissed to Billets. Capt. J.S. Ward proceeded to forward zone.	
do.	2-3-18	10am	Lt Col BARKLEY J. proceeded to take command of 2/2nd H.C. Fd Amb. Capt. J.S. Ward to be I/c 2/3rd H.C.F.A. during his absence.	
do.	3-3-18	10am	Capt. Ward J.S. proceeded to A.D.S. FARGNIERS. Personnel sent from H.Q.'s to relieve personnel in the line. Lt Wilson M.O.R.C. relieved Lt. Bean.	
		3pm	Lt McBean M.O.R.C. + 3 O.R. proceeded for course of instruction at Fifth Army R.A.M.C. school.	
do.	4-3-18	11am	50 men sent as a working party to make a new Collecting Post at VOUEL Sht. 66c. T.19.c.6.2.	
do.	4-3-18	10am	Lieut Dowling M.O.R.C. posted to 2/2 London Regt for temporary duty.	
do.	5-3-18	10am	Lt Cavanagh posted to 58 D.A.C. for temporary duty.	
do.	7-3-18	10am	Lt Lees M.O.R.C. relieved Lt Cavanagh as M.O. to 58 D.A.C.	
do.	10-3-18	9.30am	C.O. inspected work at New Collecting Post, VOUEL. Reported to A.D.M.S. that D 290 Batty R.F.A. were making emplacements for guns 50 yds distance on either side of the post.	
do.	11-3-18	10am	C.O. to forward area with A.D.M.S. 58 Division.	
do.	12-3-18	10am	C.O. inspecting work at New Collecting Post VOUEL.	
do.	13-3-18		Relay Post at TRAVECY Sht. 66c. U.1.a.7.3 evacuated. All personnel + equipment withdrawn.	
do.	13-3-18	2pm	C.O. attending Conference at CHAUNY.	
		5pm	Lt CAVANAGH M.O.R.C. proceeded for duty as Medical Officer to 58 Div. Machine Gun Batt.	
			Lt McBean rejoined from course of instruction at School of Sanitation PERONNE.	
do.	14-3-18	10am	C.O. to forward Area.	

Instructions regarding War Diaries and Intelligence Summaries are contained in F. S. Regs., Part II. and the Staff Manual respectively. Title Pages will be prepared in manuscript.

WAR DIARY
or
~~INTELLIGENCE SUMMARY~~

(Erase heading not required.)

Army Form C. 2118.

2/3RD HOME COUNTIES FIELD AMBULANCE.

Place	Date	Hour	Summary of Events and Information	Remarks and references to Appendices
MAREST DAMPCOURT Sh 70c 6.7 b 3.0	14.3.18		During night of 14/15 march 1918 A.D.S. being withdrawn from FARGNIERS Sht 66. T.27.b.9.9 & opened at VOUEL Sht 66c T.19.c.6.2. Site of old A.D.S T.27.b.9.9. being used as a relay Post manned by 1 N.C.O. & 8 other ranks. [initials]	
do	15.3.18	9 am	Completion of move of Advanced Dressing Stations. [initials]	
		9 pm	Medical Arrangements for Keeps received. Supply of boxes to be handed over to 173rd Bde containing comforts & dressings. Boxes to be sealed & labelled + Medical Emergency box. Boxes will not be opened until absolutely necessary. [initials]	
do	16.3.18	9.30 am	CO to forward area. [initials]	
do	18.3.18		Boxes – Medical Emergency handed over to HQ's 173rd I Bde [initials]	
do	20.3.18	noon	Lt Col BARKLEY J rejoined and took over command of the Unit	
		3 pm	Capt J S WARD RAMC T rejoined 2/1st H.C. Field Ambulance.	
		4.30 pm	Order received from ADMS 58th Division "Prepare for battle". CO to forward area.	
		8 pm	All Ambulance Cars sent forward 2 large & 2 Fords at ADS & 3 large at CHAUNY.	
CHAUNY			Hdqrs transferred to CHAUNY. All available men held in readiness as [illegible]. [initials]	
	21.3.18	3 am	Information received enemy using gas on left division.	
		5 am	Order received from ADMS 58th Divn to occupy battle positions.	
		7.20 am	O/c ADS VOUEL reports some shelling of VIRY – TERGNIER Road, otherwise all correct. No casualty passed through up to present.	
		9 am	Information received that 41 C.C.S CHAUNY was closed, also Advanced Operating Theatre Abbecourt. All leave cancelled. [initials]	

2449 Wt. W14957/M90 750,000 1/16 J.B.C. & A. Forms/C.2118/12.

Instructions regarding War Diaries and Intelligence Summaries are contained in F. S. Regs., Part II. and the Staff Manual respectively. Title Pages will be prepared in manuscript.

WAR DIARY
or
~~INTELLIGENCE SUMMARY~~

(Erase heading not required.)

Army Form C. 2118.

2/3RD HOME COUNTIES FIELD AMBULANCE.

Place	Date	Hour	Summary of Events and Information	Remarks and references to Appendices
CHAUNY.	21.3.18	9 am	CO to forward zone. Application from 173rd I Bde for ambulance Car – several casualties at Advanced Brigade Headquarters at QUESSY. VIRY – TERGNIER road now impassable.	
do.	21.3.18	2 pm	1 man killed 6 OR. wounded, 5 horses killed 3 wounded by shells at MAREST DAMPCOURT.	
		2.30 pm	ADS, VOUEL T 19 c 6 2 retiring to VILLEQUIER AUMONT. Sht 66c S 19 b 5 2. Personnel at R.A.P. HANGARS T 23 c 9 2 retired to VOUEL. Relay Post FARGNIERS T 27 b 9 9 evacuated and personnel retired to VOUEL.	
VILLEQUIER AUMONT. Sht 66c S 19 c 5 2.			HQ's of Unit transferred to VILLEQUIER AUMONT S.19.c 5 2. Wounded passing through ADS steadily.	
		6 pm	ADS Vouel returned to VILLEQUIER AUMONT 66c S 19 b 5 2.	
		8 pm	[illegible] Personnel arrived from MAREST DAMPCOURT. 40 Personnel from line reported to rest.	
		10 pm	40 Personnel proceeded to forward area to collect wounded. Vicinity of VOUEL very heavily shelled.	
do.	22.3.18	6 am	OC Bearers reported no wounded lying out.	
		[illegible]	Bearer Post at VOUEL evacuated as enemy advancing. ADS VILLEQUIER AUMONT retired to MAREST Sht 70c L 1 c 6 2. Wounded could be collected on lorries [illegible]. RAP located at VIRY NOREUIL. All bearers returning to MAREST DAMPCOURT. Transport retiring to BRETIGNY.	
MAREST Sht 70c L 1 c 6 2	23.3.18	9 am	Bearers sent to forward area – majority returned 3 hours later – enemy advancing. Bearer Post established at CHAUNY. Wounded passing through quickly – mostly walking wounded. 1 Ambulance driver wounded & evacuated. 1 Bearer wounded & remaining at duty.	

2449 Wt. W14957/M90 750,000 1/16 J.B.C. & A. Forms/C.2118/12.

Army Form C. 2118.

Instructions regarding War Diaries and Intelligence Summaries are contained in F. S. Regs., Part II. and the Staff Manual respectively. Title Pages will be prepared in manuscript.

WAR DIARY
~~or~~
~~INTELLIGENCE SUMMARY~~

(Erase heading not required.)

2/3RD HOME COUNTIES FIELD AMBULANCE.

Place	Date	Hour	Summary of Events and Information	Remarks and references to Appendices
MAREST SU 70 E L. 1. C. 6. 2.	21.3.18	7 am	Bearers sent to relief squads already in line. 2 squads to be located at R.A.P. CHAUNY & 1 squad at Relay Post, OGNES.	
		10 am	All bearers returned. Enemy reported having broken through our line. C.O. proceeded in direction of CHAUNY to ascertain accuracy of report.	
		11 am	Field Ambulance evacuated A.D.S. & all billets – enemy advancing. – Unit marching to VARENNES.	
VARENNES.		4 pm	Field Ambulance arrived and ordered to 'Stand by'. All official documents likely to be of use to the enemy destroyed by fire.	
do.	25.3.18	9 am	Field Ambulance vacated VARENNES & marched to NAMPCEL stopping 2 hours at CUTS en route. Arrived at NAMPCEL at 4 pm. Troops located in a cave.	
NAMPCEL	26.3.18		Unit standing by for orders.	
do.	27.3.18	8 am	Unit vacated NAMPCEL and marched to HAUTEBRAYE arriving at 1 pm.	
HAUTEBRAYE	28.3.18	2 pm	A.D.M.S. 58th Divn visited H.Q.'s. C.O. went with A.D.M.S. to HOE/B.52 at FONTENOY. Capt. JARDINE reported for duty.	
do.	29.3.18	9.30 am	Capt. JARDINE, Lt. McBEAN with personnel of 1 tent sub division proceeded for duty at HOE/B.52 at FONTENOY. This party to be rationed by this Unit.	
		10 am	Lt DOOLING F. M.O.R.C., U.S.A. proceeded for duty with 1/2nd ~~[illegible]~~ London Regt.	
do.	30.3.18	10 am	C.O. visited H.O.E./B.51.	
do.	31.3.18	am	C.O. visited H.O.E./B.57. 25 L.D. horses collected from R.A. details. 5 handed over to 2/1st H.C. F.A.	
		5 pm	A.D.M.S. 58th Divn here. All stores which we shall be unable to carry when we moved sent to H.O.E./B.57 for custody, until such time as we can collect them.	

2449 Wt. W14957/M90 750,000 1/16 J.B.C. & A. Forms/C.2118/12.

4

Instructions regarding War Diaries and Intelligence Summaries are contained in F. S. Regs., Part II. and the Staff Manual respectively. Title Pages will be prepared in manuscript.

WAR DIARY
or
~~INTELLIGENCE SUMMARY~~

(Erase heading not required.)

Army Form C. 2118.

Place	Date	Hour	Summary of Events and Information	Remarks and references to Appendices
	Apr 1918		WAR DIARY of 2/3rd HOME COUNTIES FIELD AMBULANCE. R.A.M.C., T. FROM APRIL 1ST 1918 to APRIL 30TH 1918.	Vol 15 140/2900

F. E. L. Ryles
Major ~~LIEUT.-COL.~~
O.C. 2ND/3RD HOME COUNTIES
FIELD AMBULANCE R.A.M.C.

Instructions regarding War Diaries and Intelligence Summaries are contained in F. S. Regs., Part II. and the Staff Manual respectively. Title Pages will be prepared in manuscript.

WAR DIARY
or
~~INTELLIGENCE~~ SUMMARY

(Erase heading not required.)

2/3RD HOME COUNTIES FIELD AMBULANCE.
No. ....
Date. ....

Army Form C. 2118.

Place	Date	Hour	Summary of Events and Information	Remarks and references to Appendices
HAUTEBRAYE.	1-4-18	10am	CO. visits H.O.E./B 51. at FONTENOY.	
do	2-4-18	9am	Wagon Post and Dressing Station at HAUTEBRAYE taken over from 2/1st H.C. Fd Amb.	
		10am	CO. visited H.O.E./B 51 with reference to withdrawing Personnel and stores.	
		4pm	Wagon Post and Dressing Station at HAUTEBRAYE taken over by 1/2nd H.C. Fd Amb.	
		6pm	Personnel and all stores withdrawn from H.O.E./B 51.	
do	4-4-18	10am	Field Ambulance left HAUTEBRAYE and proceeded by march route & en route for VILLERS COTTERELLS. Halted for the night at COEUVRES at 5pm	
	5-4-18	8am	Left COEUVRES & marched to VILLERS COTTERELL to ~~entrain~~	
		1pm	Entrained.	
		11pm	Detrained at LONGUEAU and marched to AMIENS.	
43 Rue Porte Paris AMIENS	6-4-18	2am	Unit arrived.	
		11.30am	Took over Corps Walking Wounded Collecting Station at 43 Rue Porte Paris, AMIENS from 72nd and 73rd Field Ambulance. ADMS. 58 Divn visited C.W.W.C. Stn. ~~67~~	
		3pm	DDMS. III Corps visited C.W.W.C. Stn. 2 Officers MORC USA reported for duty. Lt Trawin MORC & Lt Menerny M.O.R.C. Transport quartered at ECOLE de FILLES on the PICQUIGNY road.	
do	7-4-18	10am	DDMS. III Corps visited. No of patients passing through III Corps W W Stn. 67	
	9-4-18	3pm	Capt. Gilmore E.J. RAMC TC reported for duty. No of patients passing through C.W.W Stn 195	
	10.4.18		Lt J F Dooling reported for duty. No of patients passing through CWWS. 390	
	12.4.18		22 reinforcements reported for duty, includg 1 Sergt & 3 Cpls.) 1 Sgt & 2 Cpls & 4 men sent to 1/2 H.C. Fd Amb. being surplus to establishment. No of patients passed through CWWS on 11/4 203. No of patients passing through CWWS. 231.	

2449 Wt. W14957/M90 750,000 1/16 J.B.C. & A. Forms/C.2118/12.

Instructions regarding War Diaries and Intelligence Summaries are contained in F. S. Regs., Part II. and the Staff Manual respectively. Title Pages will be prepared in manuscript.

WAR DIARY
or
INTELLIGENCE SUMMARY
(Erase heading not required.)

Army Form C. 2118.

2/3RD HOME COUNTIES FIELD AMBULANCE. No. .... Date ....

Place	Date	Hour	Summary of Events and Information	Remarks and references to Appendices
43 Rue Porte Paris AMIENS	13.4.18		Number of patients passing through CWW Stn. 320.	
	14.4.18		do do. 220.	
	15.4.18		do do 188.	
		11 am	DDMS III-rd Corps visited CWW Stn	
	16.4.18		Number of patients passing through CWW Stn 164	
	17.4.18		do. do. 156	
	18.4.18		do. do. 614 Majority gassed cases.	
		9 pm	DDMS. III Corps visited CWW Stn	
	19.4.18		Number of patients passing through CWW Stn. 513 majority gassed cases { Lt. Wilson MORC sent for duty with 56	M.G. Batt.
		7 pm	DDMS. III Corps visited CWW. Stn. Arranged to send further lorries, owing to number of patients awaiting evacuation & all transport on the road evacuating.	
	20.4.18		Number of patients passing through CWW Stn. 245 large number gassed	
		11 am	DDMS III Corps visited CWW. Stn & inspected same. Also cellars under building as to their suitability as ~~their~~ for use as dressing rooms in case of bombardment.	
	21.4.18		Number of patients passing through CWW. Stn 180	
		2 pm	Lt McKinney J.B. sent for temporary duty with 2/1st H.C. Fd Amb.	
	22.4.18		Number of patients passing through CWW. Stn. 128.	
	23.4.18		Number of patients passing through CWW. Stn. 111.	
	24.4.18		Number of patients passing through CWW Stn. 1485.	
	25.4.18		Number of patients passing through CWW Stn. 853. 40 bearers sent to 2/1st H.C. F.A. for work in forward area.	

Instructions regarding War Diaries and Intelligence Summaries are contained in F. S. Regs., Part II. and the Staff Manual respectively. Title Pages will be prepared in manuscript.

WAR DIARY
or
INTELLIGENCE SUMMARY
(Erase heading not required.)

Army Form C. 2118.

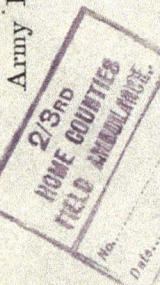

2/3RD HOME COUNTIES FIELD AMBULANCE. No. .... Date ....

Place	Date	Hour	Summary of Events and Information	Remarks and references to Appendices
43 RUE PORTE PARIS AMIENS	26.4.18		ADMS. 58 Division wounded. Lt Col. BARKLEY J. appointed Acting A.D.M.S.	
			Capt. Rogers F.E.W. to temporary command of the Unit.	
			Number of wounded passing through C.W.W. Stn. 331.	
	27.4.18		DDMS. III Corps visited C.W.W. Stn.	
			Number of wounded passing through CWW Stn. 71	
		9 pm	CWW Stn. closed for admissions.	
			Lt Mc NERNEY M.O.R.C. rejoined Unit from 2/1st H.C.F.A.	
	28.4.18	4 am	40 Bearers rejoined from 2/1st H.C. F. Amb.	
		10 am	Unit moved off from AMIENS en route for new destination.	
CROUY		4 pm	Arrived at Crouy. Unit billeted for night.	
do.	29.4.18	9 am	left CROUY for BUIGNY L'ABBE – Unit's new destination.	
BUIGNY L'ABBE		4 pm	Arrived BUIGNY L'ABBE.	
			Q.M. & Hon. Lt POOLE F. joined Unit from England.	
do.	30.4.18		C.O. departed to HQ's 58 Divn to take up duties of A.D.M.S.	
			Reception Hospital opened for 175th I. Bde group for patients who are likely to be fit for duty within 7 days.	

F.E.W. Rogers

Major
~~LIEUT. COL.~~
O.C. ~~2nd~~/3rd HOME COUNTIES FIELD AMBULANCE R.A.M.C.

2449 Wt. W14957/M90 750,000 1/16 J.B.C. & A. Forms/C.2118/12.

7

Instructions regarding War Diaries and Intelligence Summaries are contained in F. S. Regs., Part II. and the Staff Manual respectively. Title Pages will be prepared in manuscript.

WAR DIARY

~~or~~

~~INTELLIGENCE SUMMARY~~

(Erase heading not required.)

Army Form C. 2118.

2/3RD HOME COUNTIES FIELD AMBULANCE. No. Date

Place	Date	Hour	Summary of Events and Information	Remarks and references to Appendices
May 1918			WAR DIARY of 2/3RD HOME COUNTIES FIELD AMBULANCE R.A.M.C.T. FROM MAY 1ST 1918 to MAY 31ST 1918. COMMITTEE FOR MEDICAL HISTORY OF THE WAR Date 9 JUL 1918 M Berkeley LIEUT. COL. O.C. 2ND/3RD HOME COUNTIES FIELD AMBULANCE R.A.M.C.	Vol 16 140/2982

2449 Wt. W14957/M90 750,000 1/16 J.B.C. & A. Forms/C.2118/12.

Instructions regarding War Diaries and Intelligence Summaries are contained in F. S. Regs., Part II. and the Staff Manual respectively. Title Pages will be prepared in manuscript.

WAR DIARY

~~or~~

~~INTELLIGENCE SUMMARY~~

(Erase heading not required.)

Army Form C. 2118.

2/3RD HOME COUNTIES FIELD AMBULANCE.
No.............
Date...........

Place	Date	Hour	Summary of Events and Information	Remarks and references to Appendices
BUIGNY L'ABBE.	2.5.18	9 am.	Tent sub division sent to take over III rd Corps Skin Depot, ROUVROY.	JW
	4.5.18		Orders received for move of Unit to new area. Transport to proceed by road on 5.5.18 with transport of 175th I. Bde. Personnel to proceed by busses on 6th. CO. to select a site.	JW
	5.5.18	9 am.	Transport moved by road to new area with transport of 175th I. Bde. JW	
	6.5.18	7 am.	Personnel moved by route march to embussing point. – AILLY LE HAUT CLOCHER. Embussed at 10 am. debussing near CONTAY at 6 pm. Proceeded by route march to wood, near ST. GRATIEN. B.26 B.6.9. JW	
ST. GRATIEN. Sht 62D B.26 B.6.9	6.5.18	7 pm	Arrived in new area. Personnel partly under canvas and remainder under bivouacs.	JW
	7.5.18	5 pm	Tent sub division rejoined Unit from III rd Corps Skin Centre. ROUVROY. JW	
	8.5.18	10 am	Major Gawn proceeded to H.Q. 175th I. Bde to ascertain routes of evacuation and medical aid posts in the 175th I Bde area in the BAISIEUX sector. JW	
	9.5.18	9 am	1 squad of bearers sent for 24 hours duty to occupy each R.A.P in the Baisieux sector.	JW
	9.5.18	2 pm.	CO + Maj. Gawn inspected posts and routes of evacuation in the BAISIEUX sector.	JW
		10 am	2 clerks sent for record duties of 58th Divn to III rd Corps. W. W. Station JW	
	10.5.18	9 am	Major Rogers inspected posts and routes of evacuation of the 175th I. Bde in the BAISIEUX sector.	
		9 am	Working party of 20 men under a N.C.O sent for duty to III rd Corps W.W. Stn. This party to be sent until further notice.	
		11 am	D.D.M.S. 2nd Aust Corps visited Field Ambulance site.	
		6 pm	CO attended conference at Office of A.D.M.S. 58th Divn. JW	
	12.5.18	9 am	1st Lieut TRAVIS M.R.C. sent for temporary duty to 7th H.C. F. Amb. JW	
	13.5.18		Working party at III rd CWW. Stn no more required. O/c CWW. Stn very pleased with the good work this party has done. JW	

2449 Wt. W14957/M90 750,000 1/16 J.B.C. & A. Forms/C.2118/12.

Instructions regarding War Diaries and Intelligence Summaries are contained in F. S. Regs., Part II. and the Staff Manual respectively. Title Pages will be prepared in manuscript.

WAR DIARY

~~or~~

~~INTELLIGENCE SUMMARY~~

(Erase heading not required.)

Army Form C. 2118.

2/3RD HOME COUNTIES FIELD AMBULANCE.
No.
Date.

Place	Date	Hour	Summary of Events and Information	Remarks and references to Appendices
ST. GRATIEN Sh. 62ᴰ E.2[illegible]	13.5.18	[illegible] pm	Inoculation of men of Field Ambulance commenced. [initials]	
	14.5.18	11 am.	A.D.M.S. & D.A.D.M.S. 58th Divn. visited Field Ambulance site.	
		2 pm	C.O. & Major Regan visited site of M.D.S. at Vadencourt.	
		11.30 p.	O.O. 4[illegible] of A.D.M.S. 58th Divn received re relief of Field Ambulances of 47th Divn by Field Ambulances of 58th Divn. 4th London Fd Amb. to relieve 2/3 H.C. F. Amb. at their present site. and 2/1st H.C. F. Amb. to relieve 5th London Fd Amb. at the M.D.S. VADENCOURT. Relief to be completed by 6 pm 16.5.18. [initials]	
	15.5.18	~~[illegible]~~ 11 am	C.O. of 4th London F.A. inspected Field Ambulance site and spoke of arrangements re relief.	
	noon	noon.	C.O. and Lt Poole visited M.D.S. VADENCOURT.	
		12.20 pm	A.D.M.S. & D.A.D.M.S. 47th Division inspected Field Ambulance site. [initials]	
	16.5.18	8 am	Advanced Party & stores sent to take over M.D.S. VADENCOURT.	
			3. N.C.O's & 60 men sent for duty as working party to 2/1st H.C. F.A.	
		2 pm	Advanced Party of 4th London F.A. arrived to take over site.	
VADENCOURT.		2.30 p.	Main body moved off to VADENCOURT. Cpl. Vann wounded by machine gun bullet. Remd. at duty	
		4 pm	Move and relief completed. [initials]	
	17.5.18	9 am	Number of patients passing through M.D.S. 51. Lt. Dorling proceeded on 7 days special leave	
		11 am	D.D.M.S. III Corps inspected M.D.S.	
		3 pm	G.O.C. III Corps with D.D.M.S. III Corps & A.D.M.S. 58th Divn inspected M.D.S. G.O.C. expressed his appreciation of the good work done here. [initials]	
	18.5.18	9 am	Number of patients passing through M.D.S. 47.	
		3 pm	Wind storm followed by very heavy rain. One aeroplane British brought down by gale Observer & Pilot killed [initials]	

2449 Wt. W14957/M90 750,000 1/16 J.B.C. & A. Forms/C.2118/12.

Army Form C. 2118.

Instructions regarding War Diaries and Intelligence Summaries are contained in F. S. Regs., Part II. and the Staff Manual respectively. Title Pages will be prepared in manuscript.

WAR DIARY
or
~~INTELLIGENCE SUMMARY~~

(Erase heading not required.)

2/3RD HOME COUNTIES FIELD AMBULANCE.
No. ....
Date ....

Place	Date	Hour	Summary of Events and Information	Remarks and references to Appendices
VADENCOURT	19.5.18	9am	Number of patients passing through M.D.S. 40	
		11am	ADMS 58th Divn visited M.D.S.	
	20.5.18	9am	Number of patients passing through M.D.S. 52 includes 1 Prisoner of war.	
		3pm	DADMS. III Corps visited M.D.S.	
	21.5.18	9am	Number of patients passing through M.D.S. 54.	
	22.5.18	9am	Number of patients passing through M.D.S. 56.	
		12.30pm	DMS. Fourth Army with DDMS III Corps & ADMS 58th Divn visited & inspected all departments, including	
	23.5.18	9am	Number of patients passing through M.D.S. 58.	
		3pm	3 Officers collected from R.T.O. VIGNACOURT. Capt EARLY P.V. RAMC T.C. Capt Clarke. P.S. R.A.M.C. T.C. Lt Kennedy A RAMC SR. All taken on strength temporary.	
		9pm	Orders received for officers recently joined. Capt EARLY to 2/1 HCFA Capt CLARKE to 2/2 HCFA	
	24.5.18	9am	Number of patients passing through M.D.S. 33.	
		10.30am	New officers posted as follows - Capt. EARLY P.V. 2/1st H.C. F.A. Capt Clarke P.S. 2/2 H.C. F.A. Lt Kennedy A. 2/3rd H.C. F Amb. Capt Evans. G.J. posted for duty with 58th Divl. R.E.	
		11am	DDMS. III Corps visited M.D.S.	
	25.5.18	9am	No. of patients passing through M.D.S. 39 [illegible] O.C. appointed [illegible] a/ADMS until arrival of [illegible] new ADMS	
		11am	ADMS 58th Divn visited MDS	
		3pm	DDMS. III Corps visited M.D.S. LT COL WRAITH arrived a/ADMS	

2449 Wt. W14957/M90 750,000 1/16 J.B.C. & A. Forms/C.2118/12.

Instructions regarding War Diaries and Intelligence Summaries are contained in F. S. Regs., Part II. and the Staff Manual respectively. Title Pages will be prepared in manuscript.

WAR DIARY

or

~~INTELLIGENCE SUMMARY~~

(Erase heading not required.)

Army Form C. 2118.

2/3RD HOME COUNTIES FIELD AMBULANCE.
No.............
Date.............

Place	Date	Hour	Summary of Events and Information	Remarks and references to Appendices
VADENCOURT	26.5.18	9 am	Number of patients passing through M.D.S. 37.	
		10 am	A.D.M.S. 58th Divn visited Unit. (Lt Col. WRAITH) M	
do.	27.5.18	9 am	Number of ~~patients~~ passing through M.D.S. 30.	
			A.D.M.S. 58th Divn visited M.D.S. M	
do.	28.5.18	9 am	No. of patients passing through M.D.S. 31	
		2 pm	D.D.M.S. III Corps & A.D.M.S. 58th Divn visited M.D.S. M	
do.	29.5.18	9 am	Number of patients passing through M.D.S. 54.	
	29.5.18		Lt DOOLING F.J. M.O.R.C. rejoined from leave. M	
do.	30.5.18	9 am	Number of patients passing through M.D.S. 41.	
		3 pm	C.O. attended conference at Office of A.D.M.S. 58th Divn.	
		8 pm	C.O. No. 42 of A.D.M.S. 58th Divn received re move ~~[illegible]~~ and relief of Unit on 1/6/18. Unit to be relieved by 55th Field Ambulance at M.D.S. VADENCOURT. Unit on relief to march to B.20.d. M	
do.	31.5.18	11 am	Advance Party proceeded to B.20.d. to prepare site for Field Ambulance.	
		noon	O.C. 55 Field Ambulance visited M.D.S. VADENCOURT and made arrangements for the relief by his Field Ambulance at 10.30 am June 1st 1918. M	

M. Beckley

LIEUT. COL.
O.C. 2ND/3RD HOME COUNTIES
FIELD AMBULANCE R.A.M.C.

2449 Wt. W14957/M90 750,000 1/16 J.B.C. & A. Forms/C.2118/12.

24

Instructions regarding War Diaries and Intelligence Summaries are contained in F. S. Regs., Part II. and the Staff Manual respectively. Title Pages will be prepared in manuscript.

WAR DIARY
or
~~INTELLIGENCE SUMMARY~~

(Erase heading not required.)

2/3RD HOME COUNTIES FIELD AMBULANCE. No. Date.

Army Form C. 2118.

Vol 17

Place	Date	Hour	Summary of Events and Information	Remarks and references to Appendices
June 1918			WAR DIARY of 2/3rd Home Counties Field Ambulance. R.A.M.C. T. from June 1st 1918 to June 30th 1918	140/3076.

COMMITTEE FOR THE MEDICAL HISTORY OF THE WAR
Date 7 AUG 1918

M Harkley
LIEUT. COL.
O.C. 2nd/3rd HOME COUNTIES FIELD AMBULANCE R.A.M.C.

2449 Wt. W14957/M90 750,000 1/16 J.B.C. & A. Forms/C.2118/12.

Instructions regarding War Diaries and Intelligence Summaries are contained in F. S. Regs., Part II. and the Staff Manual respectively. Title Pages will be prepared in manuscript.

WAR DIARY
or
~~INTELLIGENCE SUMMARY~~
(Erase heading not required.)

2/3RD HOME COUNTIES FIELD AMBULANCE.
No. ....
Date ....

Army Form C. 2118.

Place	Date	Hour	Summary of Events and Information	Remarks and references to Appendices
VADENCOURT.	1-6-18	10.30am	Main Dressing Station handed over to O.C. 55 Field Ambulance.	
		1pm	Personnel marched to Wood at ST GRATIEN. Sht. 62d B26 b 6 9.	
		4.15pm	Move of Unit completed.	
ST GRATIEN WOOD Sht. 62d B26 b 6 9.	2-6-18	9am	1st Lieut. Dooling J.F. M.O.R.C. detailed to look after and take Medical charge of 58th Div. Amb. Coy.	
		9am	Cpl. Lea S.R. proceeded to report to O.C. 4th Intelligence Corps Coy. with a view to transfer to Intelligence Corps.	
		3pm	Capt. PARKER detailed to take over Medical Charge of 291st Bde R.F.A. in relief of Capt. CARSWELL who will join this Unit for duty on relief.	
do.	3-6-18		Lt. Col. BARKLEY J. granted 14 days leave to England via BOULOGNE - 4/6/18 to 18/6/18. Major FEW ROGERS to command the Unit during Lt. Col. Barkley's absence.	
do.	4-6-18	10am	D.D.M.S. III Corps visited Camp.	
		10am	Capt CARSWELL R.A.M.C. T. reported for duty.	F.E.W.R.
do.	5-6-18	5.30am	C.O. inspected forward area and routes of evacuation of right Divl front of III rd Corps front.	F.E.W.R.
do.	6-6-18	5pm	A.D.M.S. 58th DIV. visited camp.	F.E.W.R.
do.	7-6-18	3pm	G.O.C., 58th DIV. inspected all horses, transport + camp of Unit. Congratulated O.C. on the cleanliness of the wagons and horses and camp.	F.E.W.R.
do.	8-6-18	11am	Divl. Gas Officer inspected the box respirators of the personnel of the Field Ambulance.	F.E.W.R.
		2pm	Capt CARSWELL R.A.M.C. T. departed for duty with Fifth Army School of Musketry.	F.E.W.R.
do.	11-6-18	3am	Orders received for move of Unit to new area.	F.E.W.R.
		6.30am	Personnel marched off en-route for embussing point - VILLERS-BOCAGE — TALMAS road.	F.E.W.R.
		8.30am	Transport moved off to join 174th Bde transport en route for new area	F.E.W.R.

2449 Wt. W14957/M90 750,000 1/16 J.B.C. & A. Forms/C.2118/12.

Instructions regarding War Diaries and Intelligence Summaries are contained in F. S. Regs., Part II. and the Staff Manual respectively. Title Pages will be prepared in manuscript.

WAR DIARY
or
INTELLIGENCE SUMMARY
(Erase heading not required.)

2/3RD HOME COUNTIES FIELD AMBULANCE.
No.........
Date.........

Army Form C. 2118.

Place	Date	Hour	Summary of Events and Information	Remarks and references to Appendices
ST. PIERRE à GOUY	11-6-18	2.50pm	Personnel arrived	
		6.50pm	Transport arrived.	F.E.G.R.
do.	12-6-18		Hospital opened for reception of sick of 174th I. Bde who are likely to be fit for duty within 4 days.	F.E.G.R.
do.	12-6-18		A.D.M.S. 58th Divn. visited C.O.	F.E.G.R.
do.	15-6-18	11pm	174th Bde order received re move of Unit to new area. – R. sector of IIIrd Corps front. Transport marching with 174th Bde column to MOLLIENS au BOIS Area on 16th. Personnel proceeding by buses on 17th. T.O. proceeded to H.Q's, 174th I. Bde to obtain authority for transport of this Unit to leave the column at MOLLIENS au BOIS area and proceed direct the same day to the camp to be occupied by this Unit.	F.E.G.R.
		11.30pm	A.D.M.S. 58th Divn. Operation Order No. 45 received re move of Unit. Unit to take over posts on routes of evacuation on R. sector of IIIrd Corps front from 5th London Field Ambulance by midnight June 18th. 80 Bearers and all Ford Cars of 2/1st & 2/2nd H.C. Fd Amb. to be at T.O. 2/3rd H.C. Fd Amb. disposal.	F.E.G.R.
do.	16-6-18	8.30am	Transport left for new area. Lt Dowling F. detailed to attend gas course at IIIrd Corps School.	
		6pm	Buses to convey personnel to new area reported for duty. To be under orders of T.O.	F.E.G.R.
do.	17-6-18	9.30am	Personnel moved off to new area in buses.	F.E.G.R.
Sht 62d B.24.b	17-6-18	12.30pm	Move completed.	
		3pm	D.A.D.M.S. 58th Div visited Camp.	
		3.30pm	Major Rogers proceeded to forward area to arrange relief of line with the 5th London F.A.	

Army Form C. 2118.

Instructions regarding War Diaries and Intelligence Summaries are contained in F. S. Regs., Part II. and the Staff Manual respectively. Title Pages will be prepared in manuscript.

WAR DIARY
or
INTELLIGENCE SUMMARY
(Erase heading not required.)

2/3RD HOME COUNTIES FIELD AMBULANCE. No. .... Date ....

Place	Date	Hour	Summary of Events and Information	Remarks and references to Appendices
Sht 62d B 26 b.	17.6.18	9.30 pm	Party sent to forward area to hold billets etc.	
	18.6.18	8 am	Bearers sent to take over posts on routes of evacuation.	
		9 am	Party sent to take over A.D.S.	7E.6.R.
Sht 62d D 15 d. 8.2.		noon	Relief on routes of evacuation and at A.D.S. completed. Hdqts located at A.D.S. Sht. 62d. D.15. d. 8 2.	
	19.6.18	7.30 am	O/c inspected forward area & posts on routes of evacuation.	7E.6.R.
		3 pm	A.D.M.S., 58th Divn. visited A.D.S.	7E.6.R.
	20.6.18	9 am	Handed over command of A.D.S. to Major GAMM F.	7E.6.R.
Sht 62d B 26 b.		noon	Hdqts transferred to ST GRATIEN WOOD Sht 62d B.26.b.	
do.	21.6.18	6.30 am	C.O. proceeded with A.D.M.S. to inspect routes of evacuation.	7E.6.R.
do	21.6.18	noon	A.D.S. heavily shelled with gas shell. A.D.S. evacuated by order of A.D.M.S. 58th DIV & re-opened at FRANVILLERS. All personnel of A.D.S. relieved as all slightly gassed.	7E.6.R.
		11 pm	Major Rogers & Capt Spencer with new staff opened A.D.S. FRANVILLERS.	7E.6.R.
do.	22.6.18	6 pm	Lt Col. BARKLEY J. rejoined from leave & took over command of Unit.	
		8 pm	Lt KENNEDY A. detailed to take over medical charge of 7/10th London Regt. until return of Lt Dooling from gas course. Lt. EATON M.O. i/c 7/10th London Regt temporarily attached to this unit - suffering slightly from effects of gas. A.D.S. closed at FRANVILLERS and reopened at D.15 d. 8 2.	
		11 pm	Lt DOOLING F. rejoined from gas course. JB	
do	24.6.18	6.30 am	CO & Lt. POOLE F. proceeded to forward area to inspect A.D.S. & routes of evacuation. Lt DOOLING F. detailed to relieve Lt KENNEDY as M.O. i/c 7/10th London Regt. JB	

2449 Wt. W14957/M90 750,000 1/16 J.B.C. & A. Forms/C.2118/12.

Army Form C. 2118.

WAR DIARY
or
INTELLIGENCE SUMMARY
(Erase heading not required.)

Instructions regarding War Diaries and Intelligence Summaries are contained in F. S. Regs., Part II. and the Staff Manual respectively. Title Pages will be prepared in manuscript.

2/3RD HOME COUNTIES FIELD AMBULANCE.
No.........
Date.........

Place	Date	Hour	Summary of Events and Information	Remarks and references to Appendices
SH. 62d B.21.7	26.6.18	7am	CO proceeded to forward area to reconnoitre new routes of evacuation.	
	26.6.18	11pm	OO. 45 of ADMS 58th DIV received. Re move of 2/2nd HCFA. to ST GRATIEN WOOD. Working party of 1 NCO. & 25 men to be supplied to dig in & revet tents also 2 Ambulance wagons & 1 G.S to report to O/c 2/2nd HCFA at 9.30am 27.6.18 for duty.	
	28.6.18	7am	C.O. visited A.D.S.	
		10am	C.O. attended conference at ADMS., 58th DIV.	
		1pm	Personnel proceeded to FRANVILLERS WOOD to prepare new Camp site.	
		2pm	CO & Major Gamm proceeded to FRANVILLERS WOOD.	
	29.6.18	11am	C.O. visited new Camp at FRANVILLERS WOOD.	
	30.6.18		Lt DOWLING F. relieved as M.O. i/c 2/10th London Regt & rejoined Unit, by Lt. EATON M.O.R.C.	

[signature]
LIEUT. COL.
O.C. 2ND/3RD HOME COUNTIES FIELD AMBULANCE R.A.M.C.

2449 Wt. W14957/M90 750,000 1/16 J.B.C. & A. Forms/C.2118/12.

19

Instructions regarding War Diaries and Intelligence Summaries are contained in F. S. Regs., Part II. and the Staff Manual respectively. Title pages will be prepared in manuscript.

WAR DIARY
or
INTELLIGENCE SUMMARY.
(Erase heading not required.)

Army Form C. 2118.

Vol 18

Place	Date	Hour	Summary of Events and Information	Remarks and references to Appendices
	July 1918			

14/3/5

2/3RD HOME COUNTIES FIELD AMBULANCE.
No.
Date

WAR DIARY

of

2/3RD HOME COUNTIES FIELD AMBULANCE. R.A.M.C., T.

FROM 1ST JULY. 1918 to 31ST JULY. 1918

CONFIDENTIAL.

COMMITTEE FOR THE MEDICAL HISTORY
Date
C SEP

Hartley
... Lieut. Col.
O.C. 2nd/3rd HOME COUNTIES FIELD AMBULANCE R.A.M.C.

Aug. 1st 1918.

D. D. & L., London, E.C.
(A8004) Wt. W1771/M2 31 750,000 5/17 Sch. 52 Forms/C2118/14

Instructions regarding War Diaries and Intelligence Summaries are contained in F. S. Regs., Part II. and the Staff Manual respectively. Title pages will be prepared in manuscript.

WAR DIARY

or

[redacted].

(Erase heading not required.)

Army Form C. 2118.

2/3RD HOME COUNTIES FIELD AMBULANCE.
No. ....
Date ....

Place	Date	Hour	Summary of Events and Information	Remarks and references to Appendices
Sht. 62D. B.26.b.6.9. ST. GRATIEN WOOD. Sht. 62D. C.20.b.4.2. FRANVILLERS WOOD.	1.7.18	2 pm	Personnel of Unit less transport moved with Headquarters to FRANVILLERS WOOD Sht. 62D C.20.b.4.2.	
		4.30pm	Move completed. Headquarters established at FRANVILLERS WOOD. Sht. 62D C.20.b.4.2. Wagon lines remain at ST. GRATIEN WOOD. Sht. 62D B.26.b.6.9. MJ	
do.	3.7.18	6.30am	CO. visited posts on routes of evacuation. MJ	
do.	4.7.18	10am	Major GRIMM. F. attended F.G.C.M. to give evidence in two cases of alleged S.I.W. of 2 men of 140th Inf Bde, 47th DIVN. MJ	
		4. 12pm.	D.D.M.S., IIIrd CORPS visited camp. MJ	
do.	5.7.18	11am	D.A.D.M.S. 58th DIV. visited camp. MJ	
		6pm	3 American Officers (medical) of 33rd American Division reported for a three days course of instruction in the duties of Medical Officers at a R.A.P. and A.D.S.	
			1st Lieut TRAVIS M.O.R.C. rejoined Unit from 2/4th London Regt. MJ	
do.	6.7.18	7am	CO visited A.D.S. and posts on routes of evacuation. MJ	
do.	7.7.18		Lieut. COOMBES. M.O.R.C. attached 2/1st H.C.Fd. Amb. reported at A.D.S for a instruction in of the duties of medical Officers at a R.A.P. and A.D.S. MJ	
do.	8.7.18	7am	CO. visited A.D.S. and posts on routes of evacuation. MJ	
		9am	Major ROGERS. F.E.W. granted 14 days leave to England via BOULOGNE MJ	
		11am	A.D.M.S. 58th Divn letter No. M.4998 received re 'Battle Station Practice.'	
		9pm	Message "Battle Station Practice" received. Capt Gilmour. R.A.M.C.T.C. with personnel proceeded to man the Walking Wounded Post. Personnel at all R.A.P's strengthened. 20 squads of reserve bearers reported at H.Q.'s. Posts all fully manned as pre-arranged plan at 1.10 am, July 9th. MJ MJ	

D. D. & L., London, E.C.
(A8004) Wt. W1771/M2 31 750,000 5/17 Sch. 53 Forms/C2118/14

Instructions regarding War Diaries and Intelligence Summaries are contained in F. S. Regs., Part II. and the Staff Manual respectively. Title pages will be prepared in manuscript.

WAR DIARY
or
~~INTELLIGENCE SUMMARY~~.
(Erase heading not required.)

Army Form C. 2118.

2/3RD HOME COUNTIES FIELD AMBULANCE.
No. ....
Date. ....

Place	Date	Hour	Summary of Events and Information	Remarks and references to Appendices
Sht 62D C 20 b.4.2 FRANVILLERS WOOD.	7.7.18	2.25am	Message "Normal dispositions" received from A.D.M.S. 58th Div.	
		4 am	All extra personnel withdrawn from posts.	
do.	8.7.18		3 American Medical Officers attached for 3 days course of instruction returned to their Unit	
do.	9.7.18	6 pm	3 American Medical Officers, 33rd American Division reported for a 3 days course of instruction in the duties of a Medical Officer at a RAP and ADS. C.O. visited forward area.	
do.	10.7.18		1st Lt DOOLING, J.F. M.O.R.C. returned for duty from 2/2nd H.C.Fd. Ambulance	
do.	11.7.18	9 am	1st Lt. DOOLING J.F. M.O.R.C. detailed to take over medical charge of 3rd London Regt during the absence of the Medical Officer on leave. C.O. visited forward area.	
do.	12.7.18	7 am	C.O. visited forward area and routes of evacuation	
		11 am	D.D.M.S., 58th Divn visited C.O.	
do.		3 pm	Lt Coombes M.O.R.C. rejoined 2/1st H.C.F.A.	
do.	13.7.18	11 am	C.O. visited A.D.M.S. 58th Division	
		1 pm	Lieut. T. J. GILMORE R.A.M.C. T.C. departed for duty with 5 C.C.S.	
		6 pm	A.D.M.S. + D.A.D.M.S. 58th Divn visited Camp. C.O. to forward area.	
do.	14.7.18	10 am	C.O. to forward area + A.D.S. G.O.C. 58th DIVN. inspected A.D.S.	
		5 pm.	C.O. visited A.D.M.S. 58th Divn.	
		5 pm	American Medical Officers attended presentation of medals at BEAUCOURT. C.O. appointed by D.M.S. Fourth Army A/A.D.M.S. 58th Divn during absence of A.D.M.S. on leave.	
do.	16.7.18	9 am	A/A.D.M.S. reconnoitred the forward zone.	
		3 pm	A/A.D.M.S. reconnoitred new routes of evacuation in the event of a general withdrawal to the second line, i.e. BAIZIEUX system.	
do.	17.7.18	6.30am	A/A.D.M.S. accompanied by Lt. Col. Hamilton visit the forward area and inspected RAP's relay posts, and A.D.S. Reconnoitred routes of evacuation in the event of a withdrawal	

D. D. & L., London, E.C.
(A8004) Wt. W1771/M2 31 750,000 5/17 Sch. 52 Forms/C2118/14

Army Form C. 2118.

WAR DIARY
or
~~INTELLIGENCE SUMMARY.~~
(Erase heading not required.)

Instructions regarding War Diaries and Intelligence Summaries are contained in F. S. Regs., Part II. and the Staff Manual respectively. Title pages will be prepared in manuscript.

Place	Date	Hour	Summary of Events and Information	Remarks and references to Appendices
Sht 62D C.20.b.4.2.	17.7.18.		to the BAIZIEUX system – from C.10.c.2.5 to the Red Chateau, MONTIGNY. [initials]	
FRANVILLERS WOOD do	18.7.18	7am	O/A.D.M.S. visited forward area.	
		8pm	1 officer, 1 N.C.O. + 8 men of American E. Force reported to A.D.S. for instruction in duties at R.A.P.'s, relay posts + A.D.S. [initials]	
do	19.7.18	8am	Work at Walking Wounded Post Sht 62D D.19.d.5.4 completed. Working Party returned to Unit.	
		8am	All personnel at A.D.S. and on routes of evacuation relieved by personnel from H.Q.'s. 1st Lieut. J.F. DOOLING M.O.R.C. evacuated sick to 1/2nd H.C. Fd. Amb. [initials]	
do	20.7.18		O/A.D.M.S. visited forward area. [initials]	
do	21.7.18	6am	D.D.M.S. III rd Corps visited posts on routes of evacuation and A.D.S. with [illegible] Hammerton [initials]	
		10am	D.D.M.S. III rd Corps inspected cookhouses and Q.M. stores at Headquarters. [initials]	
do	22.7.18	9am	O/A.D.M.S. visited forward zone. [initials]	
		6pm	O/A.D.M.S. proceeded to H.Q.'s 58th Division.	
		7pm	A.A.+Q.M.G. 58th Division visited Headquarters + inspected cookhouses + the Q.M. Stores. [initials]	
do	23.7.18	7am	O/A.D.M.S. visited forward area.	
		2pm	1 M.O. 1 N.C.O. + 8 men American E. Force returned to ~~[illegible]~~ their Units. [initials]	
do	24.7.18	11am	D.A.D.M.S. 58th Div. visited C.O.	
		9.30pm	40 extra stretcher bearers proceeded to A.D.S. to reinforce personnel at posts. [initials]	
do	25.7.18	7am	Lt. Poole proceeded to A.D.S. for duty.	
		9.30am	Lt. GALLOWAY, R.A.M.C. reported for duty at Walking Wounded Post.	
		9am	O/A.D.M.S. proceeded to A.D.S.	
		9am	40 stretcher bearers of 2/1st H.C.F.A. reported at Walking Wounded Post. These bearers are in reserve. [initials]	

D. D. & L., London, E.C.
(A8004) Wt. W1771/M2 31 750,000 5/17 Sch. 52 Forms/C2118/14

Instructions regarding War Diaries and Intelligence Summaries are contained in F. S. Regs., Part II. and the Staff Manual respectively. Title pages will be prepared in manuscript.

WAR DIARY
or
~~INTELLIGENCE SUMMARY.~~
(Erase heading not required.)

2/3RD HOME COUNTIES FIELD AMBULANCE.
No. ....
Date ....

Army Form C. 2118.

Place	Date	Hour	Summary of Events and Information	Remarks and references to Appendices
Sht 62d C 20 b 4.2 FRANVILLERS Wood.	25 7 18	5 pm	Lt Poole returned to Headquarters.	
			Major F E W ROGERS rejoined Unit from leave	
		11 am	A/A.D.M.S. reconnoitred new brigade front - left of present line - to ascertain medical arrangements and route of evacuation.	
		5.40 pm	All casualties reported clear of battle field. C.O. returned to Headquarters.	
		6 pm	A/A.D.M.S. proceeded to H.Q's. 58th Division.	
		[illegible]	All [illegible] rejoined Headquarters of their Unit. [initials]	
do.	26 7 18	10 am	Major Rogers F.E.W. relieved Major F. [illegible] as i/c A.D.S.	
		9 pm	Col. Thomson i/c 14th Aust Field Ambulance visited C.O. and made arrangements for relief to commence at 10 am July 27th 1918. [initials]	
do.	27 7 18	10 am	i/c [illegible] Tunnelling Coy visited C.O. re supplying working party for work at Medical Post at D.30. a. 9.3. 3 N.C.O.'s & 42 men required. Arrangements made for this party to be supplied. [initials]	
		2.45 pm	Completed take over of route of evacuation from 14th Aust. Field Ambulance. [initials]	
do.	28 7 18	7 am	A/A.D.M.S. visited forward area. [initials]	
		8 am	Working Party commenced work at Medical Post. D.30 a. 9.3. [initials]	
do.	29 7 18	10 am	Col. [illegible] attached A.D.M.S. 58th Divn. for instruction, visited C.O. [initials]	
do.	30 7 18	8 am	Working party commenced work at Walking Wounded Post D.17 d 5.4. [initials]	
	30 7 18	7 am	A/A.D.M.S. visited forward area.	
		11 am	D.A.D.M.S. 58th Divn. visited C.O. [initials]	
do.	31 7 18	2 pm	Capt. T.J. GILMORE RAMC TC. rejoined Unit from No 41 C.C.S. [initials]	

D. D. & L., London, E.C.
(A8004) Wt. W1771/M2 31 750,000 5/17 Sch. 52 Forms/C2118/14

11

Army Form C. 2118.

Instructions regarding War Diaries and Intelligence Summaries are contained in F. S. Regs., Part II. and the Staff Manual respectively. Title pages will be prepared in manuscript.

WAR DIARY
or
INTELLIGENCE SUMMARY.
(Erase heading not required.)

2/3RD HOME COUNTIES FIELD AMBULANCE

No. ...

Date. ...

Vol 19

Place	Date	Hour	Summary of Events and Information	Remarks and references to Appendices

Aug. 1918.

CONFIDENTIAL

140/3200.

WAR DIARY

of

2/3RD HOME COUNTIES FIELD AMBULANCE. R.A.M.C. T.

FROM AUGUST 1ST 1918 to AUGUST 31ST 1918

COMMITTEE FOR MEDICAL HISTORY OF THE WAR

Date 5 OCT. 1918

[signature]

LIEUT. COL.

O.C. 2ND/3RD HOME COUNTIES FIELD AMBULANCE R.A.M.C.

D. D. & L., London, E.C.
(A6004) Wt. W1771/M2 31 750,000 5/17 Sch. 52 Forms/C2118/14

Instructions regarding War Diaries and Intelligence Summaries are contained in F. S. Regs., Part II. and the Staff Manual respectively. Title pages will be prepared in manuscript.

WAR DIARY
or
~~INTELLIGENCE SUMMARY.~~
(Erase heading not required.)

Army Form C. 2118.

2/3RD HOME COUNTIES FIELD AMBULANCE.
No.........
Date.........

Place	Date	Hour	Summary of Events and Information	Remarks and references to Appendices
ROUND WOOD. Sh 62 C 20 b 4.2	1.8.18	7am	Lieut. Kennedy RAMC with 1 other rank proceeded as Advanced Party to new area	
		9am	CO visited forward area.	
		2pm	% 38th Field Ambulance visited CO to make arrangements for relief of line on	
			August 2nd 1918. Arranged for relief to commence at 2.30pm. JW	
	[illegible]	[illegible]	Relief of line commenced and completed at [illegible]pm.	
		[illegible]	[illegible] personnel and cars returned from doing duty in forward zone. JW	
	[illegible]	[illegible]	[illegible] moved off under Major Gamm to new area.	
		[illegible]	[illegible] handed over to % 38th Field Ambulance	
		[illegible]	CO and motor Transport proceeded to new area. JW	
VIGNACOURT		2pm	CO and motor transport arrived. All billets taken over from %	
			38th Field Ambulance in this area	
			[illegible] 58th Divn visited CO [illegible] to stand by ready to move at short	
			notice.	
		[illegible]	Transport personnel arrived	
		[illegible]	CO, GO of ADMS 58th Divn received re move of Unit to forward zone	
			on [illegible]. JW	
	[illegible]	[illegible]	[illegible] detrained at VIGNACOURT JW	
	[illegible]	[illegible]	Unit moved off by [illegible] to ST. GRATIEN WOOD	
		11pm	Move completed JW	

D. D. & L., London, E.C.
(A8094) Wt. W1771/M1231 750,000 5/17 Sch. 52 Forms/C2118/14

Instructions regarding War Diaries and Intelligence Summaries are contained in F. S. Regs., Part II. and the Staff Manual respectively. Title pages will be prepared in manuscript.

WAR DIARY
or
INTELLIGENCE SUMMARY.
(Erase heading not required.)

2/3rd HOME COUNTIES FIELD AMBULANCE. No. ...... Date ......

Army Form C. 2118.

Place	Date	Hour	Summary of Events and Information	Remarks and references to Appendices
St Gratien Wood Sht 62D 5 in B.	15.8.18		No. of patients passing through D.R.S. Admd 16. Evac. 17.	
do.	16.8.18		No of patients passing through D.R.S Admd. 35. Evac. 23. To duty. 4.	
do.	17.8.18		No of patients passing through D.R.S Admd 45 Evac. 26.	
do.	18.8.18		No. of patients passing through D.R.S. Admd. 36. Evac 27.	
do.	19.8.18		No of patients passing through D.R.S. Admd 26 Evac. 17.	
		2.30pm	Lieut LONG M.O.R.C. proceeded for Temporary duty at C.R.S.	
do.	20.8.18		No of patients passing through D.R.S. admd. 34. Evac. 28. To duty. 2.	
do.	21.8.18		No of patients passing through D.R.S admd. 27 Evac. 41 To duty 2.	
		3pm	A.D.M.S. visited Camp.	
do.	22.8.18	10am	No of patients passing through D.R.S. admd 30 Evac. 41 To duty 1	
			2 OR sent to hold Field Ambulance site at PIERREGOT	
			~~No of patients passing through D.R.S. admd 30 Evac~~	
		3pm	Orders to be prepared to move at 2 hours notice received.	
do.	23.8.18	11am	A.D.M.S. 58th Divn visited Camp	
		5pm	Lieut. Kennedy A. with 3 NCO's + 10 bearers proceeded to report to O/c M.D.S. J 36 a 6.6.	
			Lieut Dowling M.O.R.C. proceeded for temporary duty at Vadencourt as M.O. to surrounding Units.	
		3pm	Box Respirators of personnel of Unit inspected as ordinary routine prior to going into forward area	

(A8004) Wt. W1771/M2 31 750,000 5/17 Sch. 52 Forms/C2118/14
D. D. & L., London, E.C.

Instructions regarding War Diaries and Intelligence Summaries are contained in F. S. Regs., Part II. and the Staff Manual respectively. Title pages will be prepared in manuscript.

WAR DIARY
or
INTELLIGENCE SUMMARY.

(Erase heading not required.)

Army Form C. 2118.

Place	Date	Hour	Summary of Events and Information	Remarks and references to Appendices
Sheet [illegible]				
[illegible]	24.8.18	7am	O.C. received [illegible] to move and take over M.D.S. from [illegible] London F. Amb. by 6pm.	
		9am	Advanced Party moved to M.D.S.	
		noon	[illegible] personnel moving off with Transport to M.D.S. [initials]	
I [illegible]		4pm	[illegible] completed.	
do	25.8.18	[illegible]	[illegible] received for M.D.S. to move forward to site of A.D.S. I [illegible] b	
		9am	Advanced Party proceeded to new site of M.D.S.	
		noon	No. of cases passing through. 84 including [illegible] P. of War.	
		2.30pm	[illegible] proceeded to new M.D.S.	
I [illegible] b		3pm	[illegible] completed. [initials]	
do	26.8.18	[illegible]	[illegible] 58th Div. visited M.D.S.	
		noon	No. of cases passing through M.D.S. ~~[illegible]~~ 183 [initials] ~~including~~ ~~P. of War~~ [initials]	
do	27.8.18		No. of cases passing through M.D.S. 217 including 17 P. of War. [initials]	
do	28.8.18	noon	No. of cases passing through M.D.S. 210 including 12 P. of War.	
			[illegible] 58th Div. visited M.D.S. [initials]	
do	29.8.18	[illegible]	D.D.M.S. IIIrd Corps & A.D.M.S. 58th Div. visited M.D.S.	
		noon	No. of cases passing through M.D.S. 138 including 6 P. of War.	
		5pm	O.C. received [illegible] M.D.S. to move forward to site of A.D.S. at L 10 a [initials]	
do	30.8.18	7am	Advanced Party proceeded to open M.D.S. at L 10 a	
		[illegible]	[illegible] party moved off to new site of M.D.S.	
L 10 a		noon	M.D.S. receiving at new site. [initials]	

D. D. & L., London, E.C.
(A8004) Wt. W1771/M2 31 750,000 5/17 Sch. 52 Forms/C2118/14

Army Form C. 2118.

2/3RD HOME COUNTIES FIELD AMBULANCE

No. ....

Date ....

WAR DIARY
or
INTELLIGENCE SUMMARY.

(Erase heading not required.)

Instructions regarding War Diaries and Intelligence Summaries are contained in F. S. Regs., Part II. and the Staff Manual respectively. Title pages will be prepared in manuscript.

Place	Date	Hour	Summary of Events and Information	Remarks and references to Appendices
Sht 62c L 10a	30.8.18	noon	No of cases passing through M.D.S. 54 including 1 P. of War.	
		1pm	O.C. recd [ins] for move of M.D.S. to site of A.D.S. at Sht 62c H 21 b.	
do.	31.8.18	8am	Advanced party proceeded to open M.D.S. at new site.	
Sht 62c H.21.b.		10am	M.D.S. receiving. ~~Old~~ M.D.S. at old site closed down and remainder of personnel moved forward.	
do.		noon	Move completed.	
do.		noon	No of cases passing through M.D.S. 77 including 5 P. of War.	
do.		11pm	[illegible] 229 Field Ambulance visited O.C. with reference to taking over M.D.S.	

LIEUT. COL.
O.C. 2ND/3RD HOME COUNTIES
FIELD AMBULANCE R.A.M.C.

D. D. & L., London, E.C.
(A8004) Wt. W1771/M231 750,000 5/17 Sch. 52 Forms/C2118/14

14

Instructions regarding War Diaries and Intelligence Summaries are contained in F. S. Regs., Part II. and the Staff Manual respectively. Title pages will be prepared in manuscript.

WAR DIARY

~~or~~

~~INTELLIGENCE SUMMARY.~~

(Erase heading not required.)

2/3RD HOME COUNTIES FIELD AMBULANCE. No. ..... Date .....

Army Form C. 2118.

Place	Date	Hour	Summary of Events and Information	Remarks and references to Appendices

Sept. 1918.

WR 19

140/3259.

CONFIDENTIAL.

WAR DIARY.

of

2/3rd HOME COUNTIES FIELD AMBULANCE.

R.A.M.C. T.

FROM SEPT. 1ST To SEPT. 30 1918.

COMMITTEE FOR THE MEDICAL HISTORY OF THE WAR 2ND ... UNIT ...

H Heckley

LIEUT. COL. O.C. 2ND/3RD HOME COUNTIES FIELD AMBULANCE R.A.M.C.

1/10/18.

D. D. & L., London, E.C. (A8004) Wt. W1771/M2 31 750,000 5/17 Sch. 52 Forms/C2118/14

Instructions regarding War Diaries and Intelligence Summaries are contained in F. S. Regs., Part II. and the Staff Manual respectively. Title pages will be prepared in manuscript.

WAR DIARY
or
~~INTELLIGENCE SUMMARY.~~

(Erase heading not required.)

2/3RD HOME COUNTIES FIELD AMBULANCE.
No.........
Date.........

Army Form C. 2118.

Place	Date	Hour	Summary of Events and Information	Remarks and references to Appendices
Sht. 62c A.21.b MARICOURT.	1.9.18	10pm.	OO of ADMS. 58th Divn received re handing over MDS to 229 F.A. on 2/9/18.	
	2.9.18	noon	Unit relieved by 229th F.A. Relief completed noon. Unit moved into adjoining camp.	
do	6.9.18	9am	Information received that Division would probably relieve 47th Divn in the line during night of 6/7th. 1 Officer and 1 NCO to reconnoitre the routes of evacuation.	
		9.30am	Major Gamm F. & Sergt J Gibson reconnoitred the routes of evacuation.	
		11am	CO visited ADMS, 58th Divn.	
		6pm	Major Gamm returned from forward area. Sergt Gibson remaining in the line with F Amb. of 47 Divn.	
		6pm	3 squads of bearers and 1 runner posted for duty with each Battalion of 175th I Bde.	
		9pm	OO of ADMS 58th Divn received re taking over ADS & route of evacuation from 6th London F.A. by noon 7th inst.	
do Sht 62c C 20 a 9.1.	7.9.18	8am	Unit moved to take over ADS at BOUCHAVESNES Sht 62c C 20 a 9 1. Take over complete by 1pm. Major Gamm with ADS personnel proceeded to open ADS at D.22.c.0.5. 3 squads of bearers sent to forward area for duty.	

D. D. & L., London, E.C. (A8004) Wt. W1771/M2 31 750,000 5/17 Sch. 52 Forms/C2118/14

Instructions regarding War Diaries and Intelligence Summaries are contained in F. S. Regs., Part II. and the Staff Manual respectively. Title pages will be prepared in manuscript.

WAR DIARY
or
~~INTELLIGENCE SUMMARY.~~
(Erase heading not required.)

2/3RD HOME COUNTIES FIELD AMBULANCE.
No. ....
Date ....

Army Form C. 2118.

Place Sht 62c	Date	Hour	Summary of Events and Information	Remarks and references to Appendices
			Hdqrs	
C.20.a.9.1	7.9.18	3pm	Unit moved to new site of A.D.S. 2nd NCO & 1 squad of bearers stationed at Car Post, D 15. c. 4 6, became casualties, through hostile shell fire. 415135 Pte Hall F.E. killed, 2 OR wounded and (74218 Pte WATKINS E. ...) returned to duty, and 1 NCO & 1 man wounded and evacuated (415272 L Cpl BICKELL C.F. and 497617 Pte THORNTON W.G.) also (... Dr BRADFORD G.) Sunbeam Car damaged & driver wounded and evacuated at this post.	
D.15.c.0.5		6pm	Main body of Unit arrived at A.D.S.	
			Major Gamm accompanied the C.O. to the forward area. [initials]	
	8.9.18	9am	A.D.S. transferred to new site at E.14.a.8.8. Main body moved off by route march to this site. [initials]	
E.14.a.8.8		3pm	Move completed. Bearers carrying wounded straight through across country from R.A.P's to A.D.S. Intermittent shelling of batteries in the vicinity of A.D.S.	
		11pm	Squads at 2/7th London Regt's R.A.P. relieved by fresh squads from H.Q's. Bearer Relay Post established at E.10.a.2.6. - 3 squads and 1 runner with Sergt. i/c posted at this post also 1 pr of stretcher wheels. [initials]	
do	9.9.18	9am	Major Gamm and Lieut Kennedy visited all R.A.P's and Relay Posts in the forward area.	
		10am	A.D.M.S. 58th Divn. visited A.D.S. and advanced posts	
		noon	D.D.M.S. IIIrd Corps visited and inspected the A.D.S. [initials]	

D. D. & L., London, E.C.
(A8004) Wt. W1771/M2 31 750,000 5/17 Sch. 52 Forms/C2118/14

Instructions regarding War Diaries and Intelligence Summaries are contained in F. S. Regs., Part II. and the Staff Manual respectively. Title pages will be prepared in manuscript.

WAR DIARY
or
~~INTELLIGENCE SUMMARY.~~
(Erase heading not required.)

2/3RD HOME COUNTIES FIELD AMBULANCE.
No. ....
Date ....

Army Form C. 2118.

Place	Date	Hour	Summary of Events and Information	Remarks and references to Appendices
E 14 a. 6.8.	9.9.18	6 pm	Car Post at E. 15. a. 7.5. (57c 62c) withdrawn as no casualties passing through this post.	
		7 pm	CO visited the forward area's posts. JB	
do	10.9.18	3 am	Sergt. Gibson with 7 squads proceeded to reinforce Bearer Relay Post at E. 10. a. 2. 6. Given orders to either establish a Relay Post at a site selected by him or to use his bearers to collect the wounded left ~~by~~ behind by the advancing troops.	
	11 am	11 am	Adv. A.D.S. established at Car Post at E. 9. a. 2. 9. (62c) Personnel at this post 1 officer and 7 O.R.	
			A.D.M.S. 58th Divn visited A.D.S. and forward posts	
		6 pm	Recommended that 3 squads should be attached to 7/4 Suffolk Regt proceeding into the line tonight. All squads attached 174th I. Bde would be withdrawn when the Brigade was relieved from the line.	
			Sergt. Gibson and extra squads rejoined from duty in forward area. JB	
do	11.9.18	9 am	Lt. Kennedy proceeded to the forward area.	
			CO with the MO 2/24th London Regt visited all posts in the forward area.	
			Squads rejoined Unit from 174th I. Bde.	
			Weather - Very windy with heavy rainfall all morning, but cleared up by evening.	
		8 pm	Severe shelling of batteries in vicinity of A.D.S. but very few casualties amongst the gunners.	
			A number of British dead collected ~~[illegible]~~ from the Battle field in the vicinity of the A.D.S. and buried at LIERAMONT. JB	

D. D. & L., London, E.C.
(A8004) Wt. W1771/M2 31 750,000 5/17 Sch. 52 Forms/C2118/14

Instructions regarding War Diaries and Intelligence Summaries are contained in F. S. Regs., Part II. and the Staff Manual respectively. Title pages will be prepared in manuscript.

WAR DIARY
~~or~~
~~INTELLIGENCE SUMMARY.~~
(Erase heading not required.)

2/3RD HOME COUNTIES FIELD AMBULANCE.
No.............
Date.............

Army Form C. 2118.

Place Sheet 62C	Date	Hour	Summary of Events and Information	Remarks and references to Appendices
E. 14 a. 8.8.	12.9.18	9am	C.O. + Lt Kennedy visited the forward area.	
			Squad attached 1/4th London Regt. returned to H.Q.s - Unit having been disbanded.	
			Orders received for the return to the W.W.C.Stn of 2 lorries, leaving only 1 for evacuation. [initials]	
			Weather - Very stormy with a heavy wind [initials]	
do.	13.9.18	9am	C.O. visited Adv. A.D.S. to investigate a report that a Battery of 6" guns were in action within 100 yards of the Post.	
		3pm	Orders received for the Adv. A.D.S. to withdraw to E.14.b.9.3. (62C) Old site at E.9.d.1.8. would be used as a Car Post. Weather - fine [initials]	
		4pm	C.O. visited A.D.M.S. at D.H.Q.	
			o/DADMS visited A.D.S. and gave orders that all bearers + cars of 2/2 H.C.F.Amb. should be returned to their Unit, and all horse transport not required for immediate use to be sent back to a site selected by the T.O. Site selected to be in vicinity of MOISLAINS. [initials]	
		6pm	All bearers and cars of 2/2nd H.C.F.A. returned. Transport moved back to VAUX WOOD, just off the NURLU - PERONNE Road.	
			A.D.S. Adv. moved to opposite side of road and now located at E.14.b.8.5. (62C) [initials]	
	10pm		Area around A.D.S. shelled with Gas, H.E. + Shrapnel	
		3pm	DADMS, 18th Divn with several RAMC Officers visited A.D.S. and made enquiries respecting routes of evacuation. [initials]	

D. D. & L., London, E.C. (A8004) Wt. W1771/M2 31 750,000 5/17 Sch. 52 Forms/C2118/14

Instructions regarding War Diaries and Intelligence Summaries are contained in F. S. Regs., Part II. and the Staff Manual respectively. Title pages will be prepared in manuscript.

WAR DIARY

~~or~~

~~INTELLIGENCE SUMMARY.~~

(Erase heading not required.)

2/3RD. HOME COUNTIES FIELD AMBULANCE.

Army Form C. 2118.

Place Sht 62c	Date	Hour	Summary of Events and Information	Remarks and references to Appendices
E. 14. a. 8.8.	14.9.18		D.A.D.M.S. 18th Divn visited A.D.S.	
		2pm	Heavy shelling of batteries in vicinity of R.D.S.	
		8pm	Major Gamm reconnoitred new routes of evacuation from forward area.	
		10pm	Severe shelling of area around A.D.S. Adv. A.D.S. withdrawn to A.D.S. at E. 14 a. 8.8. owing to the shelling.	
			Weather – fine but a cold wind blowing all day. JG	
do.	15.9.18	9am	Major Gamm proceeded to forward area. Squads posted to 7th London Regt. for duty.	
			Bearer Relay Post established at E. 10. c. 9.9. (62c) Personnel, 2 squads, 1 runner & 1 pr. of wheels.	
			Squads attached 9th & 10th London Regts to be attached to 6th & 8th London Regts for duty. Squads attached 12th London Regt. to be returned to H.Q's.	
		6pm	A.D.M.S. 58th Divn visited A.D.S. Gave orders for Trenches around the camp to be cleaned out so as to provide protection in case of heavy shelling.	
			Lt. ~~[illegible]~~ Travis reported to 8th London Regt. for duty in relief of Lieut. Macbean who is proceeding to C.C.S. for dental treatment.	
			Weather – fine. JG	
do.	16.9.18	9am	Lieut. Kennedy visited all medical posts in the forward area.	
			Batteries in vicinity of A.D.S. intermittently shelled with gas shells.	
			Hostile aircraft dropped bombs on LIERAMONT.	
			Weather – fine. JG	

D. D. & L., London, E.C. (A8094) Wt. W1771/M2031 750,000 5/17 Sch. 52 Forms/C2118/14

Instructions regarding War Diaries and Intelligence Summaries are contained in F. S. Regs., Part II. and the Staff Manual respectively. Title pages will be prepared in manuscript.

WAR DIARY
or
~~INTELLIGENCE SUMMARY.~~
(Erase heading not required.)

2/3rd HOME COUNTIES FIELD AMBULANCE.

Army Form C. 2118.

Place Sht. 62c	Date	Hour	Summary of Events and Information	Remarks and references to Appendices
E. 14. a. 8.8.	17.9.18	3am	Very heavy thunderstorm with a strong wind. Storm lasted about 1 hour.	
		9am.	Major Gamm visited all medical posts in the forward area.	
			CO to forward area.	
		11am	ADMS 58th Divn. visited ADS and forward ambulance posts.	
		6pm	Extra squads posted in forward area for coming battle and all arrangements for the evacuation of wounded complete. 62 Bearers of 2/2nd H.C.F. Amb. reported for duty ~~and~~ held in reserve. All cars of 2/1st and 2/2nd H.C. F. Amb. reported for duty. [initials]	
	18.9.18	4am	Sergt Gibson accompanied Major Gamm to the forward area. Major Gamm responsible for the flagging of the routes of evacuation over the captured ground. [initials]	
		6am	Lieut Dooling with 1 clerk, 1 dresser & one man for the buffet proceeded and established an Adv. ADS at E 9 a. 1. 8. (62c)	
			Arrangements made whereby all stretcher cases were dealt with by 12th Divn and all walking wounded dealt with by this Unit. All stretcher cases to pass through E 9 a. 1. 8. in the first instance, then either sent to E. 14 a. 8.8. for further treatment, or evacuated direct to the MDS. [initials]	
		1am	ADMS. 58th Divn visited the ADS. and inde CO. proceeded to the line [initials]	
		10am	15 additional squads sent to forward area to carry wounded between RAPs at W 29 d 9.9 to E 10 a. 2. 6 (62c & 57c) Ford car post established at E. 10. a. 2. 6. (62c) and a large Car post at E. 9. a. 1. 8 (62c) [initials]	

D. D. & L., London, E.C.
(A8094) Wt. W1771/M2 31 750,000 5/17 Sch 32 Forms/C2118/14

Instructions regarding War Diaries and Intelligence Summaries are contained in F. S. Regs., Part II. and the Staff Manual respectively. Title pages will be prepared in manuscript.

WAR DIARY
~~or~~
~~INTELLIGENCE~~ SUMMARY.

(Erase heading not required.)

2/3RD HOME COUNTIES FIELD AMBULANCE.
No.
Date

Army Form C. 2118.

Place Sht 62c	Date	Hour	Summary of Events and Information	Remarks and references to Appendices
E 14 a 8.8	16.9.18	11 am	CO proceeded to forward area to see new medical posts which had been established. Major Gamm returned from line and reported that everything was satisfactory. Wounded passing through all posts ~~quickly~~ in large numbers but no congestion. CO returned from line at 1 pm	
		6 pm	CO proceeded again to forward area. Reported gas hanging about in Sunken Road at W.29 a. (57c) which passed through W. 30 to PEIZIERES. CO slightly gassed.	
		9 pm	16 Bearers of 2/2nd H.C.F.A. returned to Unit	
		10 pm	Major Gamm proceeded to forward area. Weather - fine from 8 am.	[initials]
do.	19.9.18	9 am	CO and Major Gamm proceeded to forward Area. Established a Car Post at W. 30 b. 5.5 with 1 large and 1 Ford car for duty.	
		6 pm	Orders received from ADMS 58th Divn to withdraw from Car Post at W. 30 b. 5.5 (57c) the large car.	
			Lieut Long proceeded for duty with 2/7th London Regt.	[initials]
do.	20.9.18		Bearers posted to Battns of 175th I. Bde and 4th Suffolk Regt	
		noon	CO proceeded to line. DADMS. 58th Divn visited ADS.	
			Information received that the attack would continue on 21st zero hour being 5.40 am.	[initials]

D. D. & L., London, E.C.
(A8004) Wt. W1771/M2 31 750,000 5/17 Sch. 52 Forms/C2118/14

Instructions regarding War Diaries and Intelligence Summaries are contained in F. S. Regs., Part II. and the Staff Manual respectively. Title pages will be prepared in manuscript.

WAR DIARY
~~or~~
~~INTELLIGENCE SUMMARY.~~
(Erase heading not required.)

2/3rd HOME COUNTIES FIELD AMBULANCE.

Army Form C. 2118.

Place. Sht 62c	Date	Hour	Summary of Events and Information	Remarks and references to Appendices
E 14 a 8.8	21-9-18	8 am	Major Gamm proceeded to line. C.O. proceeded to line at 9 am.	
		9 am	C.O. sent to A.D.M.S. for all cars of the Division as casualties had collected at McPhie's post.	
		10 am	A.D.M.S. 58th Divn visited A.D.S and McPHEE'S POST	
			2 Horsed Ambulances sent forward to evacuate walking wounded from W.30 b 1.1. Large & Ford cars clearing accumulation of cases from W.30 b 5.5 (57c) to Adv A.D.S.	
			Accumulation of cases dispersed by 11 am & wounded now passing through post in a steady stream.	
		9 pm	Orders received that Division would probably be relieved during night 22/23.	
do	22-9-18	noon	Squads of Bearers posted for duty with 6th 7th & 8th London Regts. C.O. proceeded to H.Q.'s 174th I. Bde.	
		4 pm	Major Rogers rejoined Unit.	
		5 pm	Orders issued that Adv A.D.S. at E 9 d 1.8 would withdraw to E.14 a 8.8	
		9 pm	Major Gamm proceeded with splints, dressings etc to PEIZIERES and there established an A.D.S. (adv) in a large Cave. Large number of cases treated by him including 10 fractured thighs.	
do	23-9-18	9 am	Warning order received that Division would now probably be relieved by 12 Divn during night 23/24.	
		9.30 am	C.O. & Major Gamm proceeded to forward area.	
		11.25 am	Report received that a large number of wounded were lying out in KILDARE AVENUE.	

D. D. & L., London, E.C.
(A8004) Wt. W1771/M2 31 750,000 5/17 Sch. 53 Forms/C2118/14

Instructions regarding War Diaries and Intelligence Summaries are contained in F. S. Regs., Part II. and the Staff Manual respectively. Title pages will be prepared in manuscript.

WAR DIARY
~~or~~
~~INTELLIGENCE SUMMARY.~~
(Erase heading not required.)

2/3RD HOME COUNTIES FIELD AMBULANCE.

Army Form C. 2118.

Place Sht 62c	Date	Hour	Summary of Events and Information	Remarks and references to Appendices
E 14 a 8.8	23.9.18		4 squads of bearers sent from HQ's to collect these cases.	
		3pm	OO received re relief of Unit by 36 FA. Relief to be complete by 10 pm.	
		6pm	Relief commenced and completed 3 am. 24.9.18. Weather - fine.	
		8pm	Major Gamm proceeded to forward area to carry out relief of forward posts.	
		10pm	Orders received from 175th I. Bde that Unit would embus on VILLERS FAUCON - LIERAMONT road at 5 am. 24th. Transport to move independently.	
		6pm	Major Rogers with 4 OR proceeded as Advanced Party to new area. - TRONES WOOD.	[initials]
do.	24.9.18	3.30 am	Personnel of Unit moved off to embussing point.	
		4am	Transport moved off to destination.	
S.28.d 6 4. Sht 57c		7am	Unit debussed at TRONES WOOD & marched to S.28.d.6.4. Sht. 57c.	
		11am	Transport arrived. ADMS. 58th Divn visited the camp.	
		6pm	Orders received to detail 1 officer & 1 OR. to proceed to AUBIGNY and there to report to DAAG. 58th Divn at the R.T.O's office. Unit would probably move on 26th.	[initials]
do.	25.9.18	9am	CO. attended conference at ADMS office.	
		9pm	Orders received from 175th I Bde re entraining for new area. Unit to entrain at EDGEHILL STATION at 10.40 am 26.9.18. Weather fine.	[initials]
do.	26.9.18	4am	Transport moved off to Edgehill Station and personnel at 6 am.	[initials]
VILLERS au BOIS	27.9.18	1am	Unit detrained at AUBIGNY Station. & proceeded at 3 am by march route to VILLERS au BOIS. arriving at 6 am. Weather - fair.	
		noon	ADMS. 58th Divn visited camp. Informed CO. Unit would take over DRS. from 2/1st FA on 30.9.18.	[initials]

(A5004) Wt. W1771/M2131 750,000 5/17 D. D. & L., London, E.C. Sch. 52 Forms/C2118/14

Instructions regarding War Diaries and Intelligence Summaries are contained in F. S. Regs., Part II. and the Staff Manual respectively. Title pages will be prepared in manuscript.

WAR DIARY
or
~~INTELLIGENCE SUMMARY.~~
(Erase heading not required.)

2/3RD HOME COUNTIES FIELD AMBULANCE

Army Form C. 2118.

Place	Date	Hour	Summary of Events and Information	Remarks and references to Appendices
VILLERS au BOIS	27.9.18	3p	CO proceeded to D.R.S. GRAND SERVINS to see D.R.S	
		9p	OO received from ADMS 58th Divn re Unit relieving 73 F.A. at D.R.S. on 30.9.18 relief to be completed by 12 noon. Weather fair JW	
do.	28.9.18	11am	CO attended conference at ADMS. Office.	
		11p	Medical Arrangements for 58th Divn in new area received.	
		4p	SM + 2 NCO proceeded to 73 F.A. for 24 hours duty. Lieut. Kennedy proceeded to 8th London Regt for duty.– Lieut. Machean passed. Lieut. Machean reported for a few days rest JW	
do.	29.9.18	9am	1 officer + 7 O.R. proceeded to 73 F.A. for duty and arrange take over.	
		[illegible]	Party sent to take over D.R.S. in the morning. Weather fair with cold wind. JW	
do.	30.9.18	8.30am	Remainder of Unit moved to D.R.S.	
		10am	Rel of complete. Location of Unit Sht 44B Q 34 a 2 5. Weather – fair with very cold wind JW	

D. D. & L., London, E.C. (A8004) Wt. W1771/M2931 750,000 5/17 Sch. 52 Forms/C2118/14

Army Form C. 2118.

6

Instructions regarding War Diaries and Intelligence Summaries are contained in F. S. Regs., Part II. and the Staff Manual respectively. Title pages will be prepared in manuscript.

WAR DIARY
or
~~INTELLIGENCE SUMMARY.~~
(Erase heading not required.)

VR 21

Place	Date	Hour	Summary of Events and Information	Remarks and references to Appendices
2/3RD HOME COUNTIES FIELD AMBULANCE. No. ..... Date.....			CONFIDENTIAL.	160/8/927
			WAR DIARY	
			of	
			2/3RD HOME COUNTIES FIELD AMBULANCE. R.A.M.C., T.	
			FROM 1ST OCTOBER to 31ST OCTOBER 1918.	

D. D. & L., London, E.C.
(A8004) Wt. W1771/M2-31 750,000 5/17 Sch. 52 Forms/C2118/14

Army Form C. 2118.

Instructions regarding War Diaries and Intelligence Summaries are contained in F. S. Regs., Part II. and the Staff Manual respectively. Title pages will be prepared in manuscript.

WAR DIARY
or
INTELLIGENCE SUMMARY.
(Erase heading not required.)

Place	Date	Hour	Summary of Events and Information	Remarks and references to Appendices
Sht. 44E. Q.34.a.2.5.	1.10.18	9am	Patients remaining in D.R.S. 78 including 7 wounded.	
		3pm	Lieut J.F. DOOLING MORC proceeded for temporary duty with 2/2 London Regt.	
			A.D.M.S. 58th Divn inspected D.R.S.	
			Weather – very cold.	
do.	2.10.18	9am	Patients remaining in D.R.S. 90 including 7 wounded.	
			Weather – fine but very cold wind.	
do.	3.10.18	9am	Patients remaining in D.R.S. 99 including 7 wounded.	
			Weather – fine, but very cold wind.	
do.	4.10.18	9am	Patients remaining in D.R.S. 144 including 30 wounded.	
		11am	A.D.M.S. 58th Divn visited D.R.S. Informed C.O. that D.D.M.S. VIII Corps would probably inspect D.R.S. on 5th inst.	
			Weather – fine – wind not so cold as yesterday.	
do.	5.10.18	9am	Patients remaining in D.R.S. 160 including 34 wounded.	
			Weather – fine.	
do.	6.10.18	9am	Patients remaining in D.R.S. 180 including 36 wounded.	
		11am	A.D.M.S. 58th Divn inspected D.R.S.	
			Weather – fine – very cold wind.	
do.	7.10.18	9am	Patients remaining in D.R.S. 171 including 35 wounded.	
			Weather – fine.	

D. D. & L., London, E.C.
(A8004) Wt. W1771/M2 31 750,000 5/17 Sch. 52 Forms/C2118/14

Instructions regarding War Diaries and Intelligence Summaries are contained in F. S. Regs., Part II. and the Staff Manual respectively. Title pages will be prepared in manuscript.

WAR DIARY
or
~~INTELLIGENCE SUMMARY.~~

(Erase heading not required.)

Army Form C. 2118.

Place	Date	Hour	Summary of Events and Information	Remarks and references to Appendices
SW 44 Q 34 a 2 5.	8.10.18	9am	Patients remaining in DRS. 215 including 36 wounded.	
		6pm	ADMS 58th Divn visited DRS.	
			Weather - stormy & very cold.	
do	9.10.18	9am	Patients remaining in DRS. 212 including 36 wounded.	
		10am	DADMS. 58th Divn visited DRS.	
			Weather fine.	
do	10.10.18	9am	Patients remaining in DRS. 215 including 31 wounded.	
		10am	GOC 58th Divn with ADMS. 58th Divn visited DRS and inspected transport of Unit.	
		3pm	DDMS VIII Corps inspected DRS.	
			Lieut [illegible] MORC. rejoined Unit from 7th London Regt.	
			Lieut [illegible] MORC. rejoined Unit from leave.	
			Weather - fair - occasional heavy storms.	
do	11.10.18	9am	Patients remaining in DRS. 206 including 34 wounded.	
		11am	Lieut [illegible] MORC. relieved Lt [illegible] MORC as MO. 1/1 3rd London Regt.	
		2pm	Lieut [illegible] MORC reported for duty.	
			Weather - fine.	
do.	12.10.18	9am	Patients remaining in DRS. 210 including 25 wounded.	
		9.20am	CO attended conference at office of ADMS. 58th Divn.	

D. D. & L., London, E.C.
(A8004) Wt. W1771/M2 31 750,000 5/17 Sch. 52 Forms/C2118/14

Instructions regarding War Diaries and Intelligence Summaries are contained in F. S. Regs., Part II. and the Staff Manual respectively. Title pages will be prepared in manuscript.

WAR DIARY
or
~~INTELLIGENCE SUMMARY.~~
(Erase heading not required.)

Army Form C. 2118.

Place	Date	Hour	Summary of Events and Information	Remarks and references to Appendices
[illegible] 24 a 2.5.	12.10.18	11am	1 officer and 10 other ranks proceeded for duty at VIII Corps Rest Station FRESNICOURT.	
			[illegible] of A.D.M.S. 58th Divn received re move of D.R.S. & Unit on 13th inst. [illegible] FOSSE 10 [illegible] Move to be complete by noon.	[initials]
	13.10.18	9am	Patients remaining in D.R.S. 104 including 14 wounded. Lieut Poole F. proceeded on 14 days leave to England. [illegible] moved to new site of D.R.S.	
Sheet 44B R 8 cent.		11am	Move complete. Location R.8 cent.	
		[illegible]	A.D.M.S. 58th Divn visited D.R.S. Weather fine.	[initials]
do	14.10.18	9am	Patients remaining in D.R.S. 184 including 15 wounded.	
		5pm	D.D.M.S. Fifth Army with A.D.M.S. 58th Divn visited D.R.S. Weather fine.	
do	15.10.18	9am	Patients remaining in D.R.S. 172 including 13 wounded. [illegible] proceeded for temporary duty with 2/1st H.C.F. Amb. Weather fine.	[initials]
do	16.10.18	9am	Patients remaining in D.R.S. including wounded. Lieut Long & party rejoined Unit from VIII Corps Rest Station	[initials]

D. D. & L., London, E.C.
(A8094) Wt. W1771/M2-31 750,000 5/17 Sch. 52 Forms/C2118/14

Army Form C. 2118.

WAR DIARY
or
~~INTELLIGENCE SUMMARY.~~
(Erase heading not required.)

Instructions regarding War Diaries and Intelligence Summaries are contained in F. S. Regs., Part II. and the Staff Manual respectively. Title pages will be prepared in manuscript.

Place	Date	Hour	Summary of Events and Information	Remarks and references to Appendices
Sht 44 B. R. 8 cent.	17-10-18	9am	Patients remaining in Hosp. 96 including 1 wounded. weather misty clearing later. Rather cold.	
do.	18-10-18	9am	Patients remaining in Hosp 93 including 1 wounded	
		3pm	Visit by D.M.S. weather cold and clear.	
do	19-10-18	9am	Unit moved to FOUQUIERES. Rear party of 2 offs and 20 ORs left at FOSSE 10. Advance party of 4 ORs proceeded to FOUQUIERES. Patients remaining in D.R.S. 71 including 1 wounded weather clear and warmer changed to rain later.	
Sht. 44 A. O 21 a cent.	20-10-18	8am.	Unit moved to OSTRICOURT. Advance party of 1 off and 5 O.R's. Rear party of 8 O.R's left at FOUQUIERES. Patients remaining in D.R.S. 116 including 1 wounded. weather rainy.	
Sht. 44 A. P 6 a. 9. 3.	21-10.18	8am	Unit moved to BERSEE. Rear party of 2 O.Rs. left at OSTRICOURT.	
		2pm	Chateau at BERSEE taken over as D.R.S. A.D.M.S. visited DRS ~~attendance~~. Patients remaining in D.R.S. 5 including nil wounded. weather rainy changing to fine.	

D. D. & L., London, E.C. (A8094) Wt. W1771/M2 31 750,000 5/17 Sch. 52 Forms/C2118/14

Instructions regarding War Diaries and Intelligence Summaries are contained in F. S. Regs., Part II. and the Staff Manual respectively. Title pages will be prepared in manuscript.

WAR DIARY
or
~~INTELLIGENCE SUMMARY.~~
(Erase heading not required.)

Army Form C. 2118.

Place	Date	Hour	Summary of Events and Information	Remarks and references to Appendices
Sht 44 A. L21 a.4.0	22-10-18	9 am.	A.D.M.S visited D.R.S ~~attendance~~. Rear party from FOSSE 10 with the exception of 2 O.R's. return to BERSEE Rear parties also return from FOUQUIERES and OSTRICOURT. Patients remaining in D.R.S 21 including Nil wounded. Weather fine.	
do	23-10-18	9 am	Lt Dooling J. promoted Captain. U.S.M.C. Patients remaining in D.R.S 41 including 1 wounded. Weather fine changed to rain later.	
do.	24-10-18	9 am.	Lt Kennedy granted leave from 26/10/18 to 9/11/18. Lt Long reported for duty with the 8th London Rgt. and relieved Lt. Kennedy. Patients remaining in D.R.S 28 including 1 wounded. Weather rather dull.	
do.	25-10-18	9 a.m.	Patients remaining in D.R.S. 27 including Nil wounded. Weather colder. Rain in evening.	
do.	26-10-18	9 a.m.	Warning to move to RUMEGIES either 27th or 28/10/18. Patients remaining in D.R.S. 17 including Nil wounded. Weather fine.	

D. D. & L., London, E.C.
(A8004) Wt. W1771/M2 31 750,000 5/17 Sch. 52 Forms/C2118/14

Army Form C. 2118.

WAR DIARY
or
INTELLIGENCE SUMMARY.
(Erase heading not required.)

Instructions regarding War Diaries and Intelligence Summaries are contained in F. S. Regs., Part II. and the Staff Manual respectively. Title pages will be prepared in manuscript.

Place	Date	Hour	Summary of Events and Information	Remarks and references to Appendices
Sht. 44 A L21 a. 7.0	27.10.18	9am	Visit by A.D.M.S. Move cancelled pro tem. C.O. visited new site at RUMEGIES. Patients remaining in D.R.S. 31 including 1 wounded. Weather fine changed to rain at noon.	
do.	28.10.18	9am	A.D.M.S. and C.O. visited FOSSE 10. DDMS and A.D.M.S. visited BERSEE. Patients remaining in hospital. 14 including 1 wounded. Weather dull.	
do.	29.10.18	9am	Patients remaining in D.R.S. 22 including 1 wounded. Weather dull.	
do.	30.10.18	9am	C.O. takes up the duties of A/A.D.M.S. whilst Col Wraith is on leave. Major Rogers F.E.W. becomes O.C. the unit. Patients remaining in D.R.S. 31 including 1 wounded. Weather fine. Rain later.	F.E.G.R.
do.	31.10.18	9am	Patients remaining in D.R.S. 41 including 1 wounded. Weather fine.	F.E.G.R.

D. D. & L., London, E.C.
(A8004) Wt. W1771/M2 31 750,000 5/17 Sch. 52 Forms/C2118/14

14

Instructions regarding War Diaries and Intelligence Summaries are contained in F. S. Regs., Part II. and the Staff Manual respectively. Title pages will be prepared in manuscript.

WAR DIARY
or
~~INTELLIGENCE SUMMARY.~~
(Erase heading not required.)

Army Form C. 2118.

Place	Date	Hour	Summary of Events and Information	Remarks and references to Appendices
140/3401			WAR DIARY of 2/3rd HOME COUNTIES FIELD AMBULANCE. R.A.M.C., T. from NOV. 1st to NOV 30 1918 CONFIDENTIAL	22 140/3401

[signature]
LIEUT. COL.
O.C. 2nd/3rd HOME COUNTIES FIELD AMBULANCE R.A.M.C.

D. D. & L., London, E.C.
(A8004) Wt. W1771/M2 31 750,000 5/17 Sch. 52 Forms/C2118/14

Army Form C. 2118.

WAR DIARY
or
~~INTELLIGENCE SUMMARY.~~

(Erase heading not required.)

Instructions regarding War Diaries and Intelligence Summaries are contained in F. S. Regs., Part II. and the Staff Manual respectively. Title pages will be prepared in manuscript.

Place	Date	Hour	Summary of Events and Information	Remarks and references to Appendices
BERSEE.	1-11-18	09.00	Number of patients remaining in DRS. 29	
			Weather - rained all day.	
do.	2-11-18	09.00	Number of patients remaining in DRS. 65.	
			Weather - raining all day.	
do.	3-11-18	09.00	Number of patients remaining in DRS. 63.	
			ADMS. visited DRS. Weather - fair.	
do.	4-11-18	09.00	Number of patients remaining in DRS 96 Weather - very wet	
do	5-11-18	09.00	Number of patients remaining in DRS. 98 Weather - wet.	
		noon	ADMS. 58th Divn visited DRS.	
do.	6-11-18		Number of patients remaining in DRS. 81	
		23.45hr	OO 66 of ADMS. 58th Divn received re move of Unit & DRS. to AIX. Move to be completed by 4 pm 7-11-18.	
do.	7-11-18	08.00hr	Advanced Party to site of new DRS. at AIX. 11.00hrs. Main body moved off.	
AIX		15.00	Move completed. ADMS 58th Divn visited Unit. Lt. POOLE rejoined Unit from leave.	
do.	8-11-18	09.00	Number of patients remaining in DRS. NIL. Weather - fair.	
do.	9-11-18	09.00	Number of patients remaining in DRS 59. DRS. moved to the Brewery.	
			Weather fair. DADMS. 58th Divn visited Unit. Left orders for Unit and DRS. to move to RUMEGIES on 10-11-1918.	
RUMEGIES	10-11-18	09.00	Unit moved to RUMEGIES. Move complete 12.00hrs. Patients remaining 45.	
			Weather - fair	

D. D. & L., London, E.C. (A8004) Wt. W1771/M2 31 750,000 5/17 Sch. 52 Forms/C2118/14

Instructions regarding War Diaries and Intelligence Summaries are contained in F. S. Regs., Part II. and the Staff Manual respectively. Title pages will be prepared in manuscript.

WAR DIARY
or
~~INTELLIGENCE SUMMARY.~~
(Erase heading not required.)

Army Form C. 2118.

Place	Date	Hour	Summary of Events and Information	Remarks and references to Appendices
RUMEGIES	11-11-18	9 am	Unit and D.R.S moved to WIERS.	
		16.00	Orders received ~~along the column~~ en route to WIERS that the Unit would march on to PERUWELZ. Armistice declared at 11 am.	
PERUWELZ		18.00	Unit arrived at PERUWELZ and took over ECOLE INDUSTIELLE for billets and D.R.S.	
do.	12-11-18		Number of patients remaining in D.R.S 31. Weather fine. ADMS visited D.R.S.	
do.	13-11-18	09.00	Number of patients remaining in D.R.S 28. Weather – fine. ADMS 58th Division visited D.R.S.	
do.	14-11-18	09.00	Number of patients remaining in D.R.S. 24. Weather – fine.	
do.	15-11-18	09.00	Number of patients remaining in D.R.S. 25. Weather – fine.	
do.	16-11-18	09.00	Number of patients remaining in D.R.S. 30. Weather – fine. Lt. Col. BARKLEY. J. rejoined Unit and took over Command of Unit. Major F.E.W. ROGERS proceeded on leave 18/11/18 to 1/12/18. J Barkley	
do.	17-11-18	09.00	Number of patients remaining in D.R.S. 13. Weather – fine. J Barkley	
do.	18-11-18	09.00	Number of patients remaining in D.R.S. 22. Weather – fine.	
do.	19-11-18	09.00	Number of patients remaining in D.R.S. 19. Weather – fair & a very thick fog. JB	
do.	20-11-18	09.00	Number of patients remaining in D.R.S. 19. Weather – fair. JB	
do.	21-11-18	09.00	Number of patients remaining in D.R.S. 22. Weather – fair. JB	
do.	22-11-18	09.00	Number of patients remaining in D.R.S. 22. Weather – very cold.	
		11.00	ADMS 58th Division inspected Field Ambulance and transport. JB	

D. D. & L., London, E.C.
(A8004) Wt. W1771/M2 31 750,000 5/17 Sch. 52 Forms/C2118/14

Army Form C. 2118.

Instructions regarding War Diaries and Intelligence Summaries are contained in F. S. Regs., Part II. and the Staff Manual respectively. Title pages will be prepared in manuscript.

WAR DIARY
or
~~INTELLIGENCE SUMMARY.~~
(Erase heading not required.)

2/3RD HOME COUNTIES FIELD AMBULANCE
No. ______
Date ______

Place	Date	Hour	Summary of Events and Information	Remarks and references to Appendices
PERUWELZ.	23. 11. 18	09.00	Number of patients remaining in D.R.S. 28. Weather - fine, but very cold	[initials]
do.	24. 11. 18	09.00	Number of patients remaining in D.R.S. 30. Weather. fair.	
			Lieut A Kennedy rejoined Unit from 8th London Regt.	
			Lieut. ~~&~~ Maclean W.B. posted for duty to 8th London Regt. [initials]	
do.	25. 11. 18	09.00	Number of patients remaining in D.R.S. 29. Weather. fair. [initials]	
do.	26. 11. 18	09.00	Number of patients remaining in D.R.S. 40. Weather - fair. [initials]	
do.	27. 11. 18	09.00	Number of patients remaining in D.R.S. 41 Weather - fair. [initials]	
do.	28. 11. 18	09.00	Number of patients remaining in D.R.S. 29 Weather - very wet. [initials]	
			Capt. DOOLING J.F. M.O.R.C. proceeded for duty with 85th Labour ~~Group~~.	
do.	29. 11. 18	09.00	Number of patients remaining in D.R.S. 31 Weather - fair. [initials]	
do.	30. 11. 18	09.00	Number of patients remaining in D.R.S. 23. Weather - fair. [initials]	

[signature]
LIEUT. COL.
O.C. 2nd/3rd HOME COUNTIES
FIELD AMBULANCE R.A.M.C.

D. D. & L., London, E.C.
(A6094) Wt. W1771/M2 31 750,000 5/17 Sch. 52 Forms/C2118/14

Instructions regarding War Diaries and Intelligence Summaries are contained in F. S. Regs., Part II. and the Staff Manual respectively. Title pages will be prepared in manuscript.

WAR DIARY
or
INTELLIGENCE SUMMARY.
(Erase heading not required.)

2/3RD HOME COUNTIES FIELD AMBULANCE. No. Date.

Army Form C. 2118.

Place	Date	Hour	Summary of Events and Information	Remarks and references to Appendices
Dec 1918			CONFIDENTIAL.	
			WAR DIARY.	
			of	
			2/3rd HOME COUNTIES FIELD AMBULANCE. R.A.M.C. T.F.	
			FROM DECEMBER 1st 1918 to DECEMBER 31st 1918.	
			F. C. Rogers Major O.C. 2nd/3rd HOME COUNTIES FIELD AMBULANCE R.A.M.C.	

D. D. & L., London, E.C. (A8004) Wt. W1771/M2 31 750,000 5/17 Sch. 52 Forms/C2118/14

Instructions regarding War Diaries and Intelligence Summaries are contained in F. S. Regs., Part II. and the Staff Manual respectively. Title pages will be prepared in manuscript.

WAR DIARY
or
~~INTELLIGENCE SUMMARY.~~
(Erase heading not required.)

2/3RD HOME COUNTIES FIELD AMBULANCE.
No.............
Date...........

Army Form C. 2118.

Sheets 1.

Place	Date	Hour	Summary of Events and Information	Remarks and references to Appendices
PERUWELZ.	7.12.18		Lt. Col. BARKLEY. J. proceeded on 14 days leave to England. Major F.E.W. ROGERS, assumed Command of the Unit.	
do	20.12.18	12.00	G.O.C. 58th DIVN inspected cookhouse, stores (quartermaster) and ~~Detention~~ Reception Hospital of Field Ambulance.	
do.	21.12.18	11.00	G.O.C. 58th Divn with A.D.M.S. 58th Division inspected Reception Hospital of Field Ambulance.	
do.	29.12.18		10 other ranks posted for duty at LEUZE.	

F.E.W. Rogers
Major
~~LIEUT. COL.~~
O.C. 2ND/3RD HOME COUNTIES
FIELD AMBULANCE R.A.M.C.

(A6004) Wt. W1771/M2 31 750,000 5/17 D. D. & L., London, E.C. Sch. 52 Forms/C2118/14

11

Instructions regarding War Diaries and Intelligence Summaries are contained in F. S. Regs., Part II. and the Staff Manual respectively. Title pages will be prepared in manuscript.

WAR DIARY
or
~~INTELLIGENCE SUMMARY.~~
(Erase heading not required.)

58 DIV
Box 2864

Army Form C. 2118.

Place	Date	Hour	Summary of Events and Information	Remarks and references to Appendices
Jan 1919	1		WAR DIARY	88 24
			140/3490	
			of	
			2/3rd HOME COUNTIES FIELD AMBULANCE, RAMC. T.	
			FROM JANUARY 1st 1919 to JANUARY 31st 1919.	

[signature]
LIEUT. COL.
O.C. 2nd/3rd HOME COUNTIES
FIELD AMBULANCE R.A.M.C.

Army Form C. 2118.

Instructions regarding War Diaries and Intelligence Summaries are contained in F. S. Regs., Part II. and the Staff Manual respectively. Title pages will be prepared in manuscript.

WAR DIARY
or
~~INTELLIGENCE SUMMARY.~~
(Erase heading not required.)

2/8RD HOME COUNTIES FIELD AMBULANCE.

Place	Date	Hour	Summary of Events and Information	Remarks and references to Appendices
PERUWELZ.	12.1-19.		MAJOR. F. GAMM. 'M.C.' proceeded on 14 days leave to England via U.K.	
do.	14.1-19		LT. COL. J. BARKLEY. R.A.M.C.T. rejoined from leave and took over command of Unit.	
do.	17.1-19		Personnel of Unit rejoined from detached duty at LEUZE.	
do	3.1-19.		3 men (guarantee letter) proceeded for dispersal for demobilization.	
do	4.1-19		1 man (guarantee letter) proceeded for dispersal for demobilization.	
do	11-1-19		2 other ranks (schoolmaster & coalminer) proceeded for dispersal for demobilization.	
do	18.1-19		3 other ranks (1 schoolmaster & 2 guarantee letters) proceeded for dispersal for demobilization.	
do	20.1-19		12 other ranks proceeded for demobilization.	
do.	21.1-19		4 other ranks proceeded for demobilization.	
do	22.1-19.		2 other ranks proceeded for demobilization.	
do.	24-1-19.		Orders received that R.A.M.C. would in future be demobilized under orders of D.G.M.S.	

1/2/19.

J Barkley
LIEUT. COL.
O.C. 2ND/8RD HOME COUNTIES FIELD AMBULANCE R.A.M.C.

D. D. & L., London, E.C. (A8004) Wt. W1771/M231 750,000 5/17 Sch. 52 Forms/C2118/14

Instructions regarding War Diaries and Intelligence Summaries are contained in F. S. Regs., Part II. and the Staff Manual respectively. Title pages will be prepared in manuscript.

WAR DIARY
or
INTELLIGENCE SUMMARY.
(Erase heading not required.)

2/3RD HOME COUNTIES FIELD AMBULANCE.
No.
Date.

Army Form C. 2118.

Place	Date	Hour	Summary of Events and Information	Remarks and references to Appendices
	Feb. 1919		WAR DIARY of 2/3rd HOME COUNTIES FIELD AMBULANCE. R.A.M.C. From FEBRUARY 1st to FEBRUARY 28th 1919	Vol 25

F. Sam...
Major
~~LIEUT. COL.~~
2/3rd HOME COUNTIES
FIELD AMBULANCE R.A.M.C.

D. D. & L., London, E.C.
(A8004) Wt. W1771/M2 31 750,000 5/17 Sch. 52 Forms/C2118/14

Instructions regarding War Diaries and Intelligence Summaries are contained in F. S. Regs., Part II. and the Staff Manual respectively. Title pages will be prepared in manuscript.

WAR DIARY
or
~~INTELLIGENCE SUMMARY.~~
(Erase heading not required.)

2/3RD HOME COUNTIES FIELD AMBULANCE.
No.........
Date.........

Army Form C. 2118.

Place	Date	Hour	Summary of Events and Information	Remarks and references to Appendices
PERUWELZ.	3.2.19		2 Pte. Batmen demobilized.	
"	4.2-19		15 "Y" horses sent by march route to BOULOGNE for transportation to England.	
"	6.2-19		6 men demobilized.	
"	9.2.19		5 men demobilized.	
"	10.2.19		1 man demobilized	
"	11.2.19		Capt. J. R. TRAVIS. M.O.R.C. proceeded on 14 days leave to England.	
	–		LT. COL. J. BARKLEY. proceeded to Lady Michleham's Home, Cap Martin for convalescence.	
	–		Major ROGERS F.E.W. took over Command of Unit.	
"	13.2.19		20 other ranks sent for duty to 51 C.C.S. and struck off our strength.	
"	14.2.19		6 men demobilized.	
			Major ROGERS F.E.W. proceeded for dispersal for demobilization.	
			Major F. Gamm took Command of Unit.	
"	[illegible].2.19		4 men demobilized.	
"	22.2.19		6 men demobilized.	
"	24.2.19		Lieut. COMBES. attached for duty.	
"	27.2.19		6 men demobilized.	
"	28.2.19		Lieut Combes posted as M.O. i/c 175 Bde troops & struck off strength.	
			Warning Order received to be ready to move at short notice to CHAPELLE - ~~W[illegible]~~. WATTINES	

F. Gamm
Major
~~LIEUT. COL.~~
O.C. 2/3rd HOME COUNTIES
FIELD AMBULANCE R.A.M.C.

D. D. & L., London, E.C.
(A8004) Wt. W1771/M2 31 750,000 5/17 Sch. 52 Forms/C2118/14

Instructions regarding War Diaries and Intelligence Summaries are contained in F. S. Regs., Part II. and the Staff Manual respectively. Title Pages will be prepared in manuscript.

1

WAR DIARY
or
INTELLIGENCE SUMMARY
(Erase heading not required.)

Army Form C. 2118.

Vol 26

Place	Date	Hour	Summary of Events and Information	Remarks and references to Appendices
Mar 1919			WAR DIARY 140/3551 2/3RD HOME COUNTIES FIELD AMBULANCE MARCH 1919.	

17 JUL 1919

H.A. Philpot
Lt Col RAMC T.
O.C. 2nd/3rd HOME COUNTIES FIELD AMBULANCE R.A.M.C.

Army Form C. 2118.

Instructions regarding War Diaries and Intelligence Summaries are contained in F. S. Regs., Part II. and the Staff Manual respectively. Title Pages will be prepared in manuscript.

WAR DIARY
or
~~INTELLIGENCE SUMMARY~~
(Erase heading not required.)

Place	Date	Hour	Summary of Events and Information	Remarks and references to Appendices
PERUWELZ.	2.3.19		6 men demobilized.	
		noon	medical Instructions No 70 of A.D.M.S. 58th Divn received re-move of unit to CHAPELLE à WATTINES on 4th inst.	
	4.3.19	9 am	Personnel and transport moved to Chapelle à Wattines. move completed 14.00 hrs.	
CHAPELLE à WATTINES.		16.00	Capt. HIGGINS. M.O.R.C. and Capt. H.A. PHILPOT, R.A.M.C.T. joined for duty.	
do.	7.3.19		8 men demobilized.	
do.	8.3.19		18 men demobilized.	
			major F. GAMM granted 14 days special leave to England. Capt. J.R. TRAVIS. M.O.R.C. appointed acting O/c.	
do.	13.3.19		5 men demobilized.	
do.	16.3.19		13 men demobilized.	
			Lt Col. J. BARKLEY rejoined Unit from Lady Michelham's Home. & took Command of Unit.	
do.	20.3.19		Lt. Col. J. BARKLEY departed to take Command of 26. General Hospital, Etaples. Capt. Travis. acting O/c.	
do.	25.3.19		Capt. F. POOLE. R.A.M.C.T. granted 14 days special leave to England.	
			major F. GAMM. R.A.M.C.T. rejoined from leave and took over Command of Unit.	
do.	27.3.19		Major. F. GAMM. R.A.M.C. S.R. departed to report to D.D.M.S. ROUEN. for duty.	
			Lt F. KENNEDY. R.A.M.C. S.R. departed to report to A.D.M.S., TRAINS, ABBEVILLE for duty.	
			Capt. H.A. PHILPOT. R.A.M.C.T. took over Command of Unit	
do.	30.3.19		5 men demobilized. Unit now down to Cadre establishment.	
do.	3			

H A Philpot
Capt. RAMC T.

O.C. 2nd/3rd HOME COUNTIES FIELD AMBULANCE R.A.M.C.

Instructions regarding War Diaries and Intelligence Summaries are contained in F. S. Regs., Part II. and the Staff Manual respectively. Title Pages will be prepared in manuscript.

WAR DIARY

or

~~INTELLIGENCE SUMMARY~~

(Erase heading not required.)

Army Form C. 2118.

Place	Date	Hour	Summary of Events and Information	Remarks and references to Appendices
	April 1919		War Diary 2/3rd Home Counties Field Ambulance. April. 1919.	27 140/35

2/3RD HOME COUNTIES FIELD AMBULANCE. No.

O.C. 2ND/3RD HOME COUNTIES FIELD AMBULANCE R.A.M.C.

Army Form C. 2118.

Instructions regarding War Diaries and Intelligence Summaries are contained in F. S. Regs., Part II. and the Staff Manual respectively. Title pages will be prepared in manuscript.

WAR DIARY
or
~~INTELLIGENCE SUMMARY.~~
(Erase heading not required.)

Place	Date	Hour	Summary of Events and Information	Remarks and references to Appendices
CHAPELLE - A - WATTINES	16/4/19		3 men, held on cadre under GRO 6436 for sick wastage, demobilised	
CHAPELLE - A - WATTINES	28/4/19		CAPT. T. de R. COOMBES. M.C., USA – to ST. AIGNAN, FRANCE	
CHAPELLE - A - WATTINES.	30/4/19		SGT T. COOPER T4/239185 RASC H.T. demobilized on compassionate grounds.	

H. A. Philpot
Capt R.A.M.C. T.
O.C. 2nd/3rd HOME COUNTIES FIELD AMBULANCE R.A.M.C.

2/3RD HOME COUNTIES FIELD AMBULANCE.
No. ......
Date. 30/4/19.

D. D. & L., London, E.C. (A8004) Wt. W1771/M2 31 750,000 5/17 Sch. 52 Forms/C2118/14

Army Form C. 2118.

140/35 E

Instructions regarding War Diaries and Intelligence Summaries are contained in F. S. Regs., Part II. and the Staff Manual respectively. Title Pages will be prepared in manuscript.

WAR DIARY
or
INTELLIGENCE SUMMARY
(Erase heading not required.)

2/3RD HOME COUNTIES FIELD AMBULANCE. No. Date.

Place	Date	Hour	Summary of Events and Information	Remarks and references to Appendices
	May 1919		WAR DIARY 2/3 HOME COUNTIES FIELD AMBULANCE MAY 1919.	28

23 JUL 1919

2149 Wt. W14957/M90 750,000 1/16 J.B.C. & A. Forms/C.2118/12.

Army Form C. 2118.

Instructions regarding War Diaries and Intelligence Summaries are contained in F. S. Regs., Part II. and the Staff Manual respectively. Title Pages will be prepared in manuscript.

WAR DIARY
or
INTELLIGENCE SUMMARY

(Erase heading not required.)

Place	Date	Hour	Summary of Events and Information	Remarks and references to Appendices
CHAPELLE-A-WATTINES	2/5/19		Captn J.A. HIGGINS, M.C. USA to ST. AIGNAN FRANCE.	
— do — do	12/5/19		2 men demobilized	
— do —	16/5/19		CAPTN. and QM. F. POOLE returned from leave	
— do —	17/5/19		CAPTN. and QM. F. POOLE took over command of Unit.	
— do — do	20/5/19		3 men demobilized	
— do —	21/5/19		7 men demobilized	
— do — do	22/5/19		All M.T. personnel and cars withdrawn by 11th Divl M.T. Coy.	
— do — do	24/5/19		6 "1914" men demobilized	
— do —	29/5/19		4 men returned from detached duty at 51. C.C.S.	

2/3RD HOME COUNTIES FIELD AMBULANCE.
No.........
Date.........

F. Poole Capt.
O.C. 2ND/3RD HOME COUNTIES FIELD AMBULANCE R.A.M.C.

2149 Wt. W14957/M90 750,000 1/16 J.B.C. & A. Forms/C.2118/12.

To be rendered to Officers i/c Records for transmission to the War Office.

Army Form B. 158.

CAVALRY, ARTILLERY and INFANTRY only.

Regiment, etc., or Depot 2/3rd. Home Counties Field Ambulance RAMC, T.

Station Chapelle a Wattines.

Date 1st. June 1919.

2/3RD HOME COUNTIES FIELD AMBULANCE.

LIST OF OFFICERS.

* Married or Single	Officers doing duty with the Unit — NAME	Date of being taken on the strength of the Unit	Stations (if on Detachment)
	Lieut.-Colonel—		
	Majors—		
	Captains—		
M.	PHILPOT H.A.	4-3-19.	
	Lieutenants—		
	2nd Lieutenants—		
	Adjutant—		
M.	Quartermaster— POOLE F. (Captain)	29-4-18.	
	Riding Master—		
	WARRANT OFFICERS.		
	Master Gunner—		
	Serjeant-Major—		
	Bandmaster—		

OFFICERS ATTACHED.

(Including Special Reserve and Territorial Force Officers. Authority to be quoted.)

Rank	Name	Corps	Authority	Date of joining

* The letter "M" or "S" is to be placed before the names of Officers.
† For Units of Royal Artillery, Depots of all Arms and Special Reserve Units.
NOTE 1.—The word "Sick" to be inserted against the names of all Officers who are on the Sick List, and the words "Assistant Adjutant," "Instructor of Gunnery," &c., against the name of an Officer holding such an appointment.
NOTE 2.—This Return should be rendered in Duplicate by units of New Armies only.

[28] W1153/P990 500m 5/18 145 G & S 57

Forms B. 158 / 10

Officers absent on duty.

(Exclusive of seconded Officers, but including Officers posted and not joined.)

Married or Single	Rank and Name	On what duty, at what station, from what time
/		

Officers and Warrant Officers absent with Leave.

	Rank and Name	By whose permission, and date of order	On what account	From what time	To what time

Officers and Warrant Officers who have *joined* during the preceding month, showing whether from leave of absence, on appointment, &c.

	Rank and Name	Date and cause

Officers and Warrant Officers who have *quitted* during the preceding month, showing whether on leave of absence, removal, death, &c.

	Rank and Name	Date and cause
S.	Capt. J.A.Higgins, M.C., USA	To ST.AIGNAN, FRANCE 2-5-19.

Officers absent without leave.

Rank and Name	Since what time

Captain, Commanding.

O.C., 2/3rd. Home Counties Field Ambulance

www.ingramcontent.com/pod-product-compliance
Lightning Source LLC
Chambersburg PA
CBHW081425160426
43193CB00013B/2191
9781474531191